Above the Battle?
THE BIBLE AND ITS CRITICS

Above the Battle?
THE BIBLE AND ITS CRITICS

by
Harry R. Boer

William B. Eerdmans Publishing Company

Copyright © 1975, 1976, 1977 by William B. Eerdmans Publ. Co.
255 Jefferson Ave. S.E., Grand Rapids, Mich. 49503
All rights reserved
Printed in the United States of America

Portions of this book first appeared in the *Reformed Journal*.

Library of Congress Cataloging in Publication Data

Boer, Harry R
  Above the battle?

   1.   Bible—Criticism, interpretation, etc.   2.   Bible
—Inspiration.   I.   Title.
BS511.2.B63   220.6   76-57225
ISBN 0-8028-1693-2

Contents

A Question of Word Usage

The Christian community has always related the idea of infallibility to the Bible. It has not always done so in the same way. In the main, infallibility in its application to the Bible may be understood in two ways.

According to one very prevailing view infallibility means exactly the same in its application to the Bible as it does in any non-Christian usage. There is nothing spiritually or religiously distinctive about it. It simply means that there are in the Bible no contradictions, errors of fact, or inconsistencies. There are, of course, "problem passages," but these exist only because the data needed to read them correctly are wanting. God, the true Author of Scripture, cannot err or contradict himself. This view, therefore, holds to the literal infallibility of the Bible.

The other view sees the infallibility of the Bible as a dimension that can be discerned only by the truly Christian mind. It uses the word of the marketplace, but it gives it a nuance that is never understood in the marketplace. Its concern is with the certitude, the unbreakable validity, of the gospel which only faith can recognize. It holds to an infallibility that corresponds to the character of the biblical revelation which faith accepts. In this view infallibility is a word that has been baptized. When expressing its mind with carefulness and precision, therefore, it prefers the term "biblical infallibility" to "infallibility of the Bible," however much it may use the expressions interchangeably.

It is not commonly realized that this kind of understanding enjoys the support of a powerful tradition. It allies itself deeply with both New Testament and age-old theological usage. Words like faith, love, grace, covenant, peace, creation, hope, regeneration, sin, conversion, Savior, salvation are pregnant with meaning that transcends altogether their original meaning and their use outside the covenant community. Where in the marketplace of word usage does faith mean certain knowledge or hope present possession?

So it comes about that those who hold this view of scriptural infallibility, while not indifferent to clashing data and contradictory phenomena in the Bible, refuse to allow the certitude of the gospel to be obscured by them. They also decline to resort to contrived harmonizations which somehow bring common-sense disparities into the area of infallible, revealed truth.

It is a matter of urgency that the Christian community come to a common mind on the meaning of the word infallibility as a quality of Scripture. So long as many Christians insist on using this word in the same sense in which the secular community uses it, so long will brothers and sisters in the one family of faith remain divided into "Bible-believing, evangelical, conservative, born-again Christians," on the one hand, and "liberal, non-evangelical church members," on the other.

The touchstone for our relationship to God is definitely not a certain philosophy of Scripture, however devoutly held, but an embracing in faith of Jesus Christ, the fulfilment of prophecy, incarnate, crucified, risen, and, as such, Savior of the Church and Lord of All.

This booklet endeavors by reflection on two important aspects of biblical study known as lower criticism and higher criticism to make a contribution in the contemporary situation to the understanding and appreciation of Holy Scripture as Word of God.

Is Biblical Criticism
Unbiblical?

At the turn of the century the Christian church throughout the world was reeling in fierce controversy over a new approach to the study of the Bible. The historic view that the Bible was an infallibly inspired book came under severe attack as the result of learned and extensive researches into the backgrounds and origins of the books that constituted it.

The defenders of the traditional view presented a fairly homogeneous front in this struggle. There was no question about their loyalty to the historic view of Scripture or about their loyalty to the historic gospel. This was not true of many critics of the orthodox view of Scripture. Rationalistic biblical scholarship, sometimes deeply influenced by evolutionistic thinking, called into question the very heart of the gospel.

There was a third group of scholars, however, who stood firm in the Christian faith but believed that biblical studies had entered a new era with the advent of the new method of study called higher criticism. The position of the higher critics with Christian commitment was embarrassing. Religiously they stood with the defenders of the historic faith. Academically or scientifically they felt that they could not distance themselves from the method of research that the rationalists were using. Higher criticism was not only largely disowned by the defenders of orthodoxy, but it became a term of opprobrium which in effect equated it with sub-Christianity at best and with infidelity at worst.

Time, however, is a great sorter out. Today the legitimacy of higher criticism is widely accepted. That it can be wrongly used is recognized. That it is inherently incompatible with a believing study of the Bible is a view no longer held by most theologically trained people. On the contrary, many now regard the higher critical study of the Bible as the only responsible approach to the understanding of the Scriptures as a body of religious writings.

There is, however, a large section of the Christian church which has not made peace with higher criticism. In general—however unsatisfactory the designation—that part of the church known as conservative or evangelical or orthodox or fundamentalist or "Bible-believing" continues to entertain various degrees of suspicion, not to say rejection, with respect to the term and what it stands for.

The present writer belongs to such a denomination. The characteristic self-designation of the Christian Reformed Church alternates between or fuses the adjectives "conservative" and "orthodox." It is a fairly typical example of the broad, inclusive group described above. If we were to distinguish in that broad group between narrow and less judgmental attitudes to higher criticism, the Christian Reformed Church in general would be placed in the latter category, for there is in it a tradition of genuine concern for biblical scholarship and integrity. From time to time in what follows I shall use events and attitudes in the history of my own denomination as a point of departure. I am certain that many readers will recognize very close parallels within the history of their own communion.

More fundamentally, I write for all who find higher criticism either a personal or a church problem. My appeal will be to Scripture and to reason as a faculty controlled by the Holy Spirit. My purpose is to contribute to the greater opening of the Scriptures for the enrichment and larger effectiveness of the church. I write therefore for laymen no less than for the theologically trained. The Bible is a book that comes out of the believing community, was written for the believing community by members of the believing community, and therefore belongs preeminently to the believing community. The theologically trained indeed have a special responsibility to understand the issues involved in higher criticism. It is high time, however, that we make available *to the body of believers* the liberation that comes from the realization that the Bible is not only *the Book* among the many books, but also *a book* among the many books. Indeed, one will never fully see the Bible as *the* Book unless he sees its incarnation in *a* book. This, as we shall see in due course, is not catchy phraseology but theology truly so called.

Before I take hold of the subject I want to make two observations. A discussion of biblical criticism is given more pointed relevance—particularly in the

United States—by the unspeakably tragic situation in the Lutheran Church, Missouri Synod. My long exposure to Lutheran fellow believers, beginning in my naval chaplaincy days in the early 1940s and continuing to the present in this great West African church and mission area of Nigeria, leads me to contemplate with sadness these developments. In lesser degrees the same thing has happened in many other communions, not least in my own.

The only way to prevent such disruption in the life of the church is to face the situation and talk it out. The Christian Reformed Church has never done this, in spite of a seminary upheaval in 1922, a controversy in its Chicago churches in 1937, an unsuccessful charge of deviation from the strict doctrine of Scripture against the seminary president in 1958 and 1959, the loss of at least two scholars who have subsequently achieved distinction in the field of Old Testament study, and synodical study reports and decisions on scriptural infallibility in 1961 and on scriptural authority in 1971 and 1972. Ministers—in all denominations—must take more seriously the fact that although they are servants *in* the church they exercise that servanthood (ministry) as ministers *of* the Word. One is not ordained to be *minister ecclesiae* but *minister verbi Dei*.

A second preliminary observation: there is significance in the fact that this booklet is written by a missionary in active service in West Africa. It is, I believe, the duty of missionary witness, especially in its theological expression, to exert itself to spare the churches in Africa, Asia, and South America from falling heir to the troubled and disruptive history that has characterized the church in the West in her relationship to biblical criticism. There is probably no area in theological training in which proper missionary witness can so quickly and destructively succumb to sending church propaganda as the attitude that is to be taken to the Bible. This is not a question of belief versus unbelief, but of disunity within the family of faith. It has been my direct observation that such propaganda can quite easily avail itself of misrepresentation, ecclesiastical politicking, and dishonesty. These qualities, strangely, never seem far from adorning the defense of a "high view" of Scripture.

I propose to speak about biblical criticism and its relationship to the inspiration and infallibility of the Bible. It is an exercise in sheer theological irrelevance to discourse learnedly and piously on inspiration and infallibility or to speak judgingly of higher criticism while at the same time avoiding any sustained or serious concern with the massive and crucial question of biblical criticism. That, after all, is the issue in most of the concern with these two aspects of Scripture.

We shall therefore discuss the question of biblical criticism, assessing its nature, its relationship to our study of the Bible, and the meaning which it may have for achieving a scriptural understanding of the inspiration and infallibility of the Bible.

Before all else, it is necessary to know what is meant by the term "biblical criticism." As an isolated, unrelated expression it can have two meanings. It can refer to criticism that is biblical in character. It can also refer to criticism of the Bible. It is the latter meaning that is had in mind when the term "biblical criticism" is used to designate a theological discipline. Biblical criticism, in other words, is a theological activity which subjects the Bible to criticism.

It is clear that we must subject the Bible to study, whether exegetical, historical, doctrinal, comparative, or otherwise. It is not immediately clear that we must subject it to criticism. By "criticism," again, we do not mean critical study but criticism, criticism itself. It is therefore of the greatest importance to know what is meant by "criticism" in the term "biblical criticism."

The authoritative *Oxford English Dictionary* gives two basic definitions of the word. The first is: "The action of criticizing or passing judgment upon the qualities or merits of anything; especially the passing of an unfavorable judgment, fault-finding, censure." The second definition is: "The art of estimating the qualities and character of literary artistic work; the function or work of a critic."

Unfortunately, the idea has deeply taken root in the popular mind that biblical criticism has to do with criticism in the first sense of the word. This is wholly erroneous. There can be, of course, and indeed there is, such criticism of the Bible. To make or to designate such criticism, however, is not in any sense the meaning of the term "biblical criticism." It is to be understood wholly in terms of the second definition. This the *Dictionary* itself specifies when it further defines criticism as "The critical science which deals with the text, character, composition and origin of literary documents, esp. those of the Old and New Testaments."

From a purely formal point of view, therefore,

biblical criticism stands on one line with music criticism, literary criticism, and artistic criticism. From a formal theological point of view it stands on one line with the disciplines known as doctrine, exegesis, church history, and homiletics. All of these can be well or poorly pursued, but no one in his right mind would say that any of them is inherently evil.

This thought has been well put by James Orr in his major article "Criticism of the Bible" in the eminently conservative *International Standard Bible Encyclopaedia* (ISBE) of which he was the Editor-in-Chief. Speaking of higher criticism, he refers to the destructive use to which the discipline has been put again and again. Higher criticism, he writes, "while invaluable as an aid in the domain of Biblical introduction (date, authorship, genuineness, contents, destination, etc.), manifestly tends to widen out illimitably into regions where exact science cannot follow it, where, often, the critic's imagination is his only law." But this is far from disqualifying the discipline. Orr goes on, "It would be wrong, however, to deny the legitimate place of 'higher criticism' or belittle the great services it is capable of rendering because of abuses to which it is frequently liable."

The reader may ask: Do conservatives object to their theologians studying questions of "date, authorship, genuineness, contents, destination, etc." of the books of the Bible? The answer is: definitely not. But the further answer is: definitely not, *provided that* such study does not contravene the canon of the infallibility of Scripture *as conservatives define infallibility*. For most conservatives, this definition is not exhausted by but certainly includes the position taken by the Christian Reformed Synod in 1959: "that it is inconsonant with the creeds to declare or suggest that there is an area in Scripture in which it is allowable to posit the possibility of historical inaccuracies." *It is of the greatest importance to suspend judgment on this issue until the various concepts with which our discussion is concerned have been clarified.* At the same time we should remain constantly aware of it and keep it as a point of reference.

The biblical criticism that is regarded with antipathy and suspicion in the popular and, to no small extent, in the conservative theological mind is known as "higher" criticism. It is commonly forgotten not only that there is another category of criticism known as "lower" criticism, but that the "lower" is a twin brother of the "higher" criticism. Both were conceived in and have issued from the same womb. This womb is the rational human mind. The two forms of criticism are so interrelated and basic in the study of the Bible that it is impossible to use the one properly without acknowledging the legitimacy and necessity of the other. Moreover—and this is even more important from the perspective of the present discussion—both higher and lower criticism are species of the one genus known as biblical criticism. This genus from which the complementary and symbiotic twins of "lower" and "higher" criticism have issued is a mother-stock that is governed by a very specific and inalienably characteristic essence. This essence is the spirit of rational, scientific analysis uninfluenced, insofar as that is humanly possible, by dogmatic presuppositions. For the moment we will let this statement stand undeveloped and unsubstantiated. It will be established and supported again and again by illustrative material. We wish at this time simply to define the concept of biblical criticism. This we shall now further proceed to do by specifying the characteristic function of lower criticism and the characteristic function of higher criticism. We do so in the awareness that, however the *functions* of the two types of criticism may differ, they are both *governed* by an identical spirit of rational scientific inquiry.

Lower criticism is concerned with ascertaining the text of original documents that have been lost but of which copies exist. Lower criticism is therefore more commonly called textual criticism. J. Harold Greenlee in his admirable little book *Introduction to New Testament Textual Criticism* defines the science as follows: "Textual criticism is the study of copies of any written work of which the autograph (the original) is unknown, with the purpose of ascertaining the original text."

Higher criticism is concerned with the text not as a technical piece of writing but *as literature*. It inquires into the composition, style, authorship, possible sources, the history in which, and the culture out of which the text in question arose. It is therefore frequently referred to as literary, historical, source, form, and redaction criticism, depending on the emphasis of the higher criticism in question.

Of the two disciplines lower or textual criticism is obviously the more basic. In the study of the biblical writings it seeks to determine the actual verbal text of books of the Bible as originally written. It is on the basis of the text so determined that higher criticism does its work of interpretative analysis.

In view of the history of higher and lower criticism in the past one hundred years there is a profound irony in the relationship in which these two disciplines are regarded in the church. Whereas higher criticism has a bad name in large parts of the church, lower criticism has an eminently favorable name. Both kinds of criticism are governed by methods that, as we have noted, have an identical basic rational, scientific approach to their specific tasks. But this is precisely the great objection that conservatives have to higher criticism. The difference in attitude toward lower and higher criticism is therefore a puzzling circumstance and calls for examination.

In the chapters that follow biblical references will always be to the English Bible, normally in the Revised Standard Version. The Bible which the English-speaking churches know is the vernacular English Bible. Only a handful of ministers and professors have a really competent reading knowledge of the Hebrew Old Testament and the Greek New Testament. I write for the church as a whole. In the occasional references to original language word-forms, the linguistically uninformed reader should not feel left out of the discussion.

In consideration of the primary or more basic character of lower criticism in biblical study, we shall at this point suspend our concern with higher criticism and in the next two chapters focus on the lower or textual criticism of the Bible. We do this not for its own sake—interesting though it is—but because a proper discussion of higher criticism in the context of objections to it requires this.

CHAPTER TWO

The Story of the Textus Receptus

From 1495 to 1517 Gonzales Ximenes de Cisneros, better known to history as Cardinal Ximenes, worked mightily for the reform of the Church in Spain. As part of the training for a more effective priesthood he made the Scriptures the principal subject of study for intending priests. He supported this program by undertaking in 1502 the preparation of a polyglot (many-tongued) Bible. The Old Testament was to be printed in three columns: Hebrew and Greek, with the Latin Vulgate between them. The New Testament was to be printed in Greek and in Latin.

In 1515 the New Testament was ready to be published. Unfortunately for the greater fame of Ximenes, papal permission for this was not obtained until 1520, three years after his death. Meanwhile, the imminence of the event had become known in academic circles in Europe. It also reached the ear of a Swiss publisher named Froben. The news was indeed portentous. Never yet had the Greek New Testament been reduced to print. It existed exclusively in the form of handwritten copied manuscripts. Froben saw his main chance. Flourishing only sixty years after the invention of printing, he is probably the father of the modern publishing scoop. He cast about for some great authority to prepare a Greek edition of the New Testament with which to beat Ximenes to the bookstalls. His eye fell on none less than the famed Dutch scholar, Desiderius Erasmus of Rotterdam, who, it chanced, was willing to be persuaded.

Beginning work in September 1515 and using six Greek manuscripts, five of which were textually of decidedly inferior quality, Erasmus threw a Greek New Testament together in seven months' time. Only one manuscript of the book of Revelation was available and it was in part mutilated. The last six verses of the book were altogether missing. This presented no problem for Erasmus: he simply translated the missing section from the Latin Vulgate into the requisite Greek and edited the mutilations similarly. In March 1516 the New Testament in Greek was a published fact, a notable first in the history of publishing and even more in the history of the transmission of the Bible.

Academically and commercially the venture was an instant and indeed an abiding success. Three more editions followed. When the Ximenes polyglot edition finally came out, it was quite overshadowed by the edition of Erasmus. The cardinal's forces appear to have taken the Froben-Erasmus coup in good spirit. Ximenes' chief editor, Lopez de Stunica, did chide Erasmus for not including in his edition 1 John 5:7: "For there are three that bear record in heaven, the Father, the Word, and the Holy Ghost, and these are one." This verse had made its way into the text of the Vulgate from a scribe's comment in the margin of a Greek manuscript. Erasmus said that he knew of no Greek manuscript that contained the verse, but if he found one he would include the passage in the next edition. Before long Stunica came back with a Greek manuscript that had 1 John 5:7 properly in place. Erasmus suspected that the manuscript had been made to order but he dutifully fulfilled his promise when he published his third edition in 1522.

It so happens that this third edition became in due course the unquestioned basis for all translations into the vernacular languages. We hear no more about Froben. His place in Bible printing was taken by Robert Estienne (popularly known as Stephanus) in France, and by the Elzivir brothers in Holland. Their firms published the Erasmus text with some modifications drawn from new manuscript material. The Stephanus edition of 1550 became standard for Great Britain; the Elzivir second edition of 1633 became the authority on the continent.

The Erasmus-Froben happy-go-lucky publishing coup of 1516 laid the Greek textual basis for all New Testament translations in Europe and America for more than two-and-a-half centuries. The King James Version in English and Luther's famous translation in German are based squarely on the Erasmus edition as slightly modified by Stephanus and Elzivir. The latter is the text that became famous as the "Textus Receptus"—a name drawn from the Preface of the 1633 Elzivir edition: *Textum ergo habes nunc ab omnibus receptum*: "You have, thus, a text now received by all."

This story was worth telling because it shows two characteristic features of the earliest—and for many years determinative—Greek text of the New Testament. One is the haphazard and improvised manner in which it came into being; the other is the corrupt (in the sense of inaccurate) quality of the resultant versions. Thanks to the rise of lower criticism neither of these can eventuate again. But more importantly, the birth of the *Textus Receptus* made the rise of lower criticism possible and in a sense inevitable.

Erasmus had based his edition on manuscripts copied from other manuscripts in the twelfth, thirteenth, and fifteenth centuries. One of his manuscripts was of the tenth century and was valuable, but he used it only to correct an inferior twelfth-century manuscript. From 1600 on more and more manuscripts came to light. A number of them were as early as the fourth, fifth, and sixth centuries. Translations made centuries ago into Syriac, Ethiopic, and other languages became known. Patristic studies made more and more writings of the church fathers available, with their copious quotations from the Old and the New Testaments.

In time questions inevitably arose about the reliability of the *Textus Receptus.* So great, however, was the veneration in which it and the translations that had been made from it were held, that it took many years to establish the critical texts that control Bible translation today. This brings us to the subject of our immediate interest—the lower or textual criticism of the Bible.

The story of what happened between 1750 and 1885 (when the English Revised Version appeared—virtually the same as the American

Standard Version of 1901) is so complex and technical that we note here only some items of significance to elucidate what lower or textual criticism is. During these years the mounting number of manuscripts of the Greek New Testament or parts thereof called urgently for something more than a document-by-document comparative examination. What was needed was a classification of the accumulated documents into whatever groupings or "families" their distinctive peculiarities called for.

This classification was undertaken in a breakthrough manner by the German Johann Jakob Griesbach. Between 1775 and 1806, building on the indispensable work of predecessors, he divided the manuscripts of the four gospels into three major familes: the Alexandrian (Egyptian), the Western (Roman), and the Byzantine (Constantinopolitan). This was a most demanding task and required the exercise of great linguistic and literary perception. Not all manuscripts clearly belonged to one family or the other. There was extensive copying not only within families but also between families. Nevertheless, family characteristics were determined and in terms of these characteristics individual manuscripts were assigned to one family or another.

In further refining the methodology of textual criticism great names came to grace the history of the science: Lachmann, Tregelles, Tischendorf, Gregory, von Soden, and notably the great British duo, Westcott and Hort. Later textual scholars discerned four rather than three families of texts. They are the Alexandrian, Western, Caesarean (i.e. Palestinian), and Byzantine. This classification is, however, being further refined, with the propriety of the Caesarean classification being questioned. It is the judgment of scholars that the most reliable of these families is the Alexandrian. It includes the two famous fourth-century manuscripts, Codex Vaticanus and Codex Sinaiticus. Vaticanus is a bit earlier than Sinaiticus. Sinaiticus includes the entire New Testament; Vaticanus lacks 1 and 2 Timothy, Titus, Philemon, and Revelation. Codex Vaticanus is so called because it is lodged in the Vatican Library. Codex Sinaiticus derives its name from Mt. Sinai, on whose slopes was a monastery in which that most unusual manuscript hunter and discerning textual critic, Constantin Tischendorf, chanced upon the greatest find in textual critical history.

The drama of Tischendorf's discovery can be sensed from a description of it by Sir Frederick Kenyon in his *Handbook to the Textual Criticism of the New Testament*: ". . . in the course of his travels he visited the monastery of St. Catherine on Mt. Sinai. There, in a wastepaper basket containing a number of leaves of various manuscripts, destined to light the monastery fires, he chanced to notice several leaves of vellum bearing Greek writing of an extremely early type. . . ." That was the beginning in 1844 of a search that climaxed in 1859 in the same monastery with the discovery of the now famous and priceless codex later called Sinaiticus, "wrapped in a napkin." He was allowed to take it to his room, and that night, "thinking it sacrilege to sleep, he spent in transcribing the *Epistle of Barnabas* [found at the end of Sinaiticus], of which no copy in Greek was previously known to exist."

The Caesarean family is next in reliability; then comes the Western; and finally, far behind the others, the Byzantine family. The Byzantine family is of immediate interest at this point. By all odds the poorest and the least reliable of the various text families, it is also the biggest in number of manuscripts. It was this family which exclusively provided the manuscripts from which Desiderius Erasmus managed to contrive the immensely influential *Textus Receptus.* Therefore, when a person reads the Authorized or King James Version of the Bible, he is, in the New Testament portion of it, reading a translation into English of five inferior manuscripts of the least reliable family of New Testament manuscripts, inclusive of the forgery of 1 John 5:7.

How did the Byzantine text family fall so far behind the others in quality? It would appear that early scribes were often more concerned to achieve a smooth, readable text than a truly accurate one. They endeavored to combine divergent readings into, we might say, a union reading embracing the divergencies and further "to smooth away roughnesses, to remove obscurities and generally to produce an easy and flowing text" (Kenyon, p. 301). This tendency was especially strong in Antioch of Syria, which was long the theological center of the area in which the Byzantine texts developed. To Hort, Kenyon says, the word "Syrian" was, textually speaking, "a term of utmost reproach." He described the Byzantine family in its later revised and uniform text: "Entirely blameless on either literary or religious grounds as regards vulgarized or unworthy diction, yet showing no marks of either critical or spiritual insight, it presents the

New Testament in a form smooth and attractive, but appreciably impoverished in sense and force, more fitted for cursory perusal or recitation than for repeated diligent study" (p. 303).

In actual fact the *Textus Receptus* is a testimony to God's providential faithfulness in the preservation of his Word. It faithfully conveyed the message of the gospel and in all substance the words in which it was originally written. It fell short, however, of the accuracy which modern textual scholarship has enabled us to recover. The church believes the Bible to be the Word of God. We should therefore be concerned to have it in as perfect a form as when it was read in the early church with her access either to the original or to the earliest copies of it. This should especially be a matter of concern to churches which profess to believe not simply in the inspiration or even plenary inspiration of the Bible, but in its *verbal* inspiration. Even more should those who hold to such a view of inspiration be concerned about the most accurate possible determination of the text of Scripture when it is considered that they believe in a resultant Scripture that is inerrant and infallible in the literal sense of the word.

In the next chapter we shall tell fewer stories and concentrate instead on the inherent nature and character of the principles that govern lower criticism. We shall, of course, set forth the principles in question. But they are not in themselves our deepest interest. This we find in the *essential nature* of these principles. This nature or character, as we shall discover, is of a purely rational or scientific kind. For more than fifty years the Christian Reformed Church has held that a methodology of biblical study governed by principles of a purely rational or scientific character is incompatible with the nature of Scripture as objective revelation and with the nature of faith as divinely given personal commitment and trust. Yet at the same time the methodology of lower criticism has been held in the highest esteem.

We face here a most crucial problem. May the use of principles of analysis and classification which are regarded as eminently acceptable in determining the *very words* of Scripture, the *very text* of the Word of God, be forbidden in studying the *meaning of the text* so determined? More simply: if the consistent use of lower criticism is not only legitimate but praiseworthy and even necessary, why is the consistent use of higher criticism regarded with suspicion and antipathy?

CHAPTER THREE

The Lower Criticism of the Bible

In all its gathering, classifying, and interpreting of manuscripts, lower (textual) criticism has one overriding aim: to determine as closely as possible the *ipsissima verba,* the very words, in which the original manuscripts were written. In doing so it is governed by certain norms or laws, and in the present chapter we want to state what these laws are. Before doing so, we shall note some of the more outstanding problems with which New Testament lower criticism has had to deal. We shall then read about the laws governing lower criticism with more understanding and appreciation. The five examples that will be adduced constitute unusual rather than representative problems, but for that reason illustrating the better the point I shall make.

Here we want to note that the sole and exclusive purpose of lower criticism is to determine what the original author or authors actually wrote. Its purpose is not to conclude to what we believe they should have written or what squares the most with other canonical writings. The core question in all the maze of questions and problems that confront the lower critic is: What did the original author *actually write?* So far as the text of the New Testament is concerned, the results of lower critical research and study are contained in what are called "critical texts," that is, in the words of J. H. Greenlee, texts "constructed according to the principles of textual criticism." Modern translations of the Bible are based wholly on such texts. We shall see below that they have nevertheless a way of taking liberties with the critical texts.

1. *The Lord's supper in Luke.* In Matthew 26, Mark 14, and 1 Corinthians 11, as also in the celebration of communion in the church worldwide, the order of serving the elements is first the bread and then the cup. According to the authoritative manuscripts, Luke 22 constitutes a double exception to this rule. In the King James and American Standard versions the order in Luke 22:17–20 is cup-bread-cup. In the Revised Standard Version and in the New English Bible the order is cup-bread. What is the background of this difference?

In the most ancient and reliable manuscripts there are two accounts of the institution of the Lord's supper in the gospel of Luke. They are called the longer and the shorter accounts, and they are found in the Alexandrian and Western families of manuscripts respectively. The longer account has the cup-bread-cup order, the shorter the cup-bread order. We print them side by side, taking the longer account from the American Standard Version and the shorter from the Revised Standard Version (of 1946).

The two accounts are remarkably similar from 15 to 19a. At that point the shorter account breaks off. In the critical Greek texts Westcott & Hort and Nestle (25th Edition) choose the longer version but place 19b and 20 in brackets indicating that there is some question about the authenticity of the passage. The more recent United Bible Societies' *Greek New Testament* does the same in the first edition (1966), but I gather from the commentary on the third edition that the brackets have been removed by the majority of the Editorial Committee, while the minority preferred the shorter version.

Luke 22:15ff.

ASV	RSV
15 And he said unto them, With desire I have desired to eat this passover with you before I suffer; **16** for I say unto you, I shall not eat it, until it be fulfilled in the kingdom of God. **17** And he received a cup, and when he had given thanks, he said, Take this, and divide it among yourselves: **18** for I say unto you, I shall not drink from henceforth of the fruit of the vine, until the kingdom of God shall come. **19a** And he took bread, and when he had given thanks, he brake it, and gave to them, saying, This is my body	**15** And he said to them, I have earnestly desired to eat this passover with you before I suffer; **16** for I tell you I shall not eat it until it is fulfilled in the kingdom of God. **17** And he took a cup, and when he had given thanks he said, Take this, and divide it among yourselves; **18** for I tell you that from now on I shall not drink of the fruit of the vine until the kingdom of God comes. **19** And he took bread, and when he had given thanks he broke it and gave it to them, saying, This is my body.''
(19b) which is given for you: this do in remembrance of me. **20** And the cup in like manner after supper, saying, This cup is the new covenant in my blood, even that which is poured out for you.	

2. *"Son" or "God" in John 1:18?* Few verses in the gospel of John are better known than 1:18—''No one has ever seen God; the only Son who is in the bosom of the Father, he has made him known.'' Yet, as it stands, it has no textual right to be re-

garded as the proper reading. None of the great critical texts has it. Their unanimous wording is: "No one has ever seen God; the only God [or, the only begotten God] who is in the bosom of the Father, he has made him known." In his commentary on the United Bible Societies' text, Bruce Metzger writes, "A majority of the Committee regarded the reading 'only Son' or 'only begotten Son' in some manuscripts . . . to be a scribal assimilation to John 3:16, 18 and I John 4:9." One member of the Committee dissented from the majority's high endorsement of the "only God" reading, considering that it may have been a primitive transcriptional error in the Alexandrian tradition.

3. *"Church of God" or "Church of the Lord"*? A similar problem meets the lower critic in Acts 20:28. There in his farewell to the Ephesian elders Paul says, "Take heed to yourselves and to all the flock in which the Holy Spirit has made you guardians, to feed the church of the Lord which he obtained by his own blood." The accepted reading in the critical texts is "the church of God" instead of "the church of the Lord." The manuscript authority is remarkably balanced, with great codices supporting each reading. It is noteworthy, however, that both Vaticanus and Sinaiticus have "the church of God." In view of the general manuscript balance, the critical reading is based on the principle that we shall meet presently, namely that the more difficult reading is probably the true reading. The vernacular versions, however, have "the church of the Lord."

4. *Jesus' agony in the garden.* In Luke 22:43f., we read this well-known tragic description of Jesus' suffering in the Garden of Gethsemane: "And there

appeared to him an angel from heaven strengthening him. And being in an agony he prayed more earnestly; and his sweat became like great drops of blood falling down upon the ground." In the critical version of Westcott & Hort these words are bracketed, as also in that of Nestle. In the first edition of the Bible Societies' Greek text they are omitted altogether. In the third edition they appear in brackets. What is the reason for this uncertainty in the critical texts?

In his commentary on the third edition of the Bible Societies' text Metzger acknowledges that the evidence "strongly suggests that the two verses are not part of the original text of Luke." He suggests that in all likelihood "they were added from an early source, oral or written, of extra-canonical traditions concerning the life and passion of Jesus. . . . Nevertheless, after acknowledging that the passage is in all probability a later addition to the text, in view of its evident antiquity and its importance in the textual tradition, a majority of the committee decided to retain the words in the text, but to enclose them in double square brackets."

5. *Two versions of Acts.* Lastly, we note that in the ancient church two types of manuscript copies of Acts were circulating, one being of the Alexandrian, the other of the Western family of texts. The Alexandrian text is the shorter of the two and the more sober. The Western text is ten percent longer and is considered by scholars to be the more colorful and readable. In general, but only in general, the Alexandrian text is considered to be the more accurate. In numerous instances, however, the textual critics accept Western readings. So difficult is the

textual criticism of Acts that nearly one third of Metzger's commentary is devoted to Acts alone, 244 out of 769 pages. Matthew with 72 pages is the next longest.

Sometimes the apologetes for the less than perfect text of the New Testament go to great lengths to minimize the textual problems in it. It is true that scholars have approximated very close to the actual words of the original documents, but this may never close our eyes to the difficulties that remain. Further we must note that the vernacular editions do not always faithfully use the data that the scholars have established.

With this illustrative background we shall now summarize the few but formidable principles that the two great British scholars, Brooke Foss Westcott and Fenton John Anthony Hort, formulated to guide textual critics in the pursuit of their research.

The critical principles of Westcott and Hort are six in number.

1. Out of several possible readings, that reading which is the harder to understand or which seems the less natural is often to be regarded as the original wording. The reason for this is that a copyist would be more disposed to simplify a difficult reading or render it more naturally than to create a difficult reading. The more difficult reading may therefore be presumed to have survived or to have resisted simplification. It is because of this principle that the critics in a textually balanced situation, as in Acts 20:28, choose "the church of God" rather than the more expected "the church of the Lord."

2. Where a given passage has several manu-

script readings, that reading is to be preferred which appears to account best for the coming into being of the other readings.

3. Where changes are intentional (such as to make a smoother or more literary, more logical, more contextually harmonious reading) there is more likelihood that words will be added to than omitted from the original text. Therefore the shorter reading is generally to be preferred.

The above three principles are called "principles of intrinsic probability." It will be clear that in applying these principles the subjective judgment of the critic may well play a significant role. In order to reduce this element to a minimum, three further principles have been evolved.

4. The fourth principle is best given in the words of Greenlee: "It is desirable to strengthen the basis for decision by applying these principles to a large number of passages in a given manuscript so as to determine the extent to which the manuscript generally has readings which are preferred." When this is done manuscripts with a high percentage of preferred readings are probably reliable in instances where intrinsic probability is uncertain.

5. Still greater certainty will be gained when manuscripts can be classified according to their relationship to other manuscripts. This makes possible the bringing into being of manuscript families. These then indicate the family characteristics which can be looked for in as yet unclassified material or can be used to strengthen or check evaluations made only on the basis of intrinsic probability. The manuscript family will also point to a common ancestor (the ultimate ancestor being the original text).

Vaticanus and Sinaiticus clearly belong to the Alexandrian family of manuscripts. Their strong similarities point to the common ancestor. Their differences, however, indicate that each was copied from a different copy of that ancestor.

6. Having established the family likeness, greater objective criticism can in turn be brought to bear on individual manuscripts of the family. Thus the refining process continues.

In more recent development of principles underlying textual criticism, there has been a movement away from reliance on family or group witnesses to a more individual assessment of each textual problem on its own merits. This, however, involves no change in the scientific character of the approach to textual problems.

With these examples and principles now before us we wish to draw some conclusions for the Christian attitude to the Bible.

In the first place, one does not have to be an expert in the art of lower criticism to discern that lower criticism *is a science.* By that is meant, in the words of the dictionary, "a branch of study concerned with observation and classification of facts, especially with the establishment of verifiable general laws, chiefly by induction and hypothesis." A more apt description of the principles listed above can hardly be found. In all science there is a relationship between the human subject and the object under study in which the former *analyzes* and *makes judgments* about the latter.

Second, it is by such purely rational, systematic methods that lower criticism establishes the original or approximately original text of the New Testament. That the Bible is the Word of God, that it is divine revelation, that its message of salvation can be apprehended only through the illumination of the heart and mind by the Holy Spirit, has no bearing on the method, the processes, of lower criticism or on the norms by which these methods and processes are governed. The practitioners of the science of lower criticism are doubtless devout and dedicated Christian men, treating with reverence the sacred text which they study and analyze. But in their capacity as lower critics it is, again reverently speaking, a matter of indifference whether they are trying to determine the original text of a Greek play by Sophocles or of Paul's letter to the Romans. The methods, the spirit of scientific inquiry, the aims, are the same in both instances.

Third, one of the greatest objections that is raised against the use of higher criticism is that man with his limited and sinful mind sets himself above the divine revelation given in Scripture as its analyst and critic. The human may not judge the divine. Inspiration has given us an infallible, a verbally infallible Bible, and no amount of "phenomena" in the Bible (or outside of the Bible) that cannot be squared with its verbally inspired data may permit a qualification of the doctrine of infallibility. We shall return to this question later in our discussion of higher criticism and infallibility.

We must take note of this essential position at this point, however. We do so because the judging that is forbidden with respect to higher criticism is precisely what we do (with general approval) in lower criticism. And there it is not done with respect to an interpretation or particular view of a given part of Scripture, but with respect to the *very words* of Scripture. After all, it makes a difference whether Luke 22:43–44 is in the Bible or not; whether Acts is ten percent longer or shorter; whether Christ is described as only begotten Son or as only begotten God; whether the Bible says that the church was bought by the blood of God or by the blood of the Lord. The *content* of the Word of God is in these important matters determined by the judgments of men. And these men are fallible. Their judgments are arrived at in terms of "intrinsic probability" in the text; by majority and minority votes in committee. A striking instance of this is the exclusion of Luke 22:43, 44 from the first edition of the Bible Societies' text and its inclusion in the third edition (1971). The same thing happened with respect to the adulterous woman in John 7:53–8:11. One suspects that the inclusions were dictated more by external pressures than by true lower critical considerations.

Fourth, in his classic article "Criticism of the Bible" in the *International Standard Bible Encyclopaedia,* James Orr correctly observes that textual criticism "has a well-defined field in which it is possible to apply exact canons of judgment." This does not, however, alter its basically human and fallible character. It is men who discover the principles of lower criticism, and it is men who apply them. And this, let us note again, is not related to meaning, interpretation, or historical, cultural, or other kinds of relevance—in short, to man's word *about* the Bible—but it is determinative of *the text of Scripture itself.* Any errors that can be made here are, in the nature of the case, limited. Even a defective text like the *Textus Receptus* faithfully conveys the content and message of the Bible. Lower or textual criticism does, however, rest exclusively on the assumption that insofar as the Bible is a collection of human writings it may be examined and analyzed like any other piece of literature.

Does this assumption have significance for the study of the content (in distinction from the verbal text) of the Bible in its relation to the history, literature, sources, culture, and religious background in the context of which the books that constitute the Bible were written? This is the problem of higher criticism in its various forms, and it will have to be evaluated on its own merits. The late Professor Louis Berkhof, a strong opponent of higher criticism, wrote about lower criticism: "It is hardly necessary to add that the textual critic may not allow himself to be influenced by traditional views or by any dogmatic presuppositions" (*Beknopte Bijbelsche Hermeneutiek*, no date, p. 84. Translation from the Dutch by H. R. B. A subsequent abridgement in English does not contain the reference).

If lower and higher criticism are two branches of the one discipline called biblical criticism, how is the principle enunciated so clearly by Professor Berkhof to be understood in its application to higher criticism? With this problem we shall be concerned in subsequent chapters.

CHAPTER FOUR

The Humanity of the Bible

There is an interesting similarity between the natural science called biology and the theological discipline called biblical criticism. Biology divides into the two branches of zoology and botany. The first is concerned with animal life and the second with plant life. Each is a *logos* (science) about *bios* (life), and each is related to the other.

Similarly, biblical criticism divides into the two disciplines of lower criticism and higher criticism. Each is a systematic scientific inquiry into the nature of the Bible as literature. The first and more basic discipline is concerned with determining as nearly as possible the original text of the several books of the Bible. The second has to do with the authorship, date of writing, religious, cultural and historical context, purpose of writing, and literary characteristics of the text which lower criticism establishes. Lower cannot exist without higher and higher cannot exist without lower criticism.

Theological conservatives by and large heartily endorse lower criticism. Almost equally they reject higher criticism when it is applied as consistently as lower criticism. It is as though the biological scientist were heartily to endorse zoology while frowning on botany. We must now inquire into the legitimacy of this widely held distinction.

Both lower and higher criticism make this fundamental assumption about the Bible: however one may estimate its God-given character as revelation, it lies before us in the form of a thoroughly human product. It is a collection of writings which *as literary entities* have been produced by men in the same way in which any other book has been written. The fact of inspiration has much to say about the *product* of the writing; it in no way deprives the *act* of writing of its intellectual, emotional, and voluntary character. Inspiration leaves the inspired writer fully human; inspiration leaves his writing as mediated by his mind and heart and will fully human.

This assumption is wholly shared by conservatives with respect to lower (or textual) criticism—at least this would seem to be a fair conclusion from their unreserved acceptance of both its methods and its fruits.

The same assumption is either thoroughly rejected or thoroughly qualified with respect to higher criticism. There is an undefined point on the higher critical scale—varying from one evangelical community to another—beyond which, by virtue of some mystical consensus, critical inquiry may not go. This brings into being the following peculiar situation. You may say a dozen times that the Bible is God's Word, that it is a divine book, God-breathed writing, verbally inspired, infallible and inerrant, without saying a word about its human character, and your piety will never be questioned but rather praised. But if you say one time, somewhat emphatically, that the Bible is a human book, bearing all the characteristics of such origin, without immediately qualifying your remarks by mention of its divine aspect, the quality of your piety and of your reliability as a teacher of the Word of truth may be called into question.

It is of little use to talk about higher criticism, whether about its legitimacy and benefits or its misuse and dangers, without first facing this rather striking attitude in the church. It must be taken with the greatest seriousness. It has to do with the heart, the center, the all-or-nothing of the Christian faith. It has to do with the *incarnation*. God has been pleased to reveal himself in Christ as *a man.* The Word that was with God, that was God, that was in the beginning with God, through whom all things were made and without whom nothing has been made, *that* Word became flesh. In Christ the human and the divine natures exist, according to the definitive decision of the Fourth Ecumenical Council held at Chalcedon in 451, "inconfusedly, unchangeably, indivisibly, inseparably, the distinction of the natures being by no means taken away by the union, but rather the property of each nature being preserved."

What the Council meant to say by this is that the incarnation of the Son of God in the flesh of a man, of a human being, is real, is historical, and that this is a central article of faith. The flesh which he assumed is, according to the teaching of the Bible and the understanding of the church, the flesh of our humanity—weak, mortal, broken, subject to all the vicissitudes of life, to suffering and to death itself.

Specifically the biblical witness rejects the *docetic* view of Christ. This is a point of crucial significance for our understanding of the nature of the Bible and therefore needs explaining.

Strong in the early church and never wholly surrendered by the later church, the docetic view of Jesus' humanity is a subtle (and sometimes not so subtle) heresy that must always be guarded against. The word "docetic" is derived from the Greek word *dokein* meaning "to seem." Jesus "seemed" to hunger, "seemed" to suffer, "seemed" to have a natural human body, "seemed" to die, "seemed" to be truly one of us. In the docetic view therefore he neither was nor did any of these. How could the eternal Son of God become a truly human being, and suffer and die? That is docetism, the heresy which the church rejected, in spite of an innate tendency to accept it. But she rejected it because she does not live by her religious moods or sentiments or defective traditions, much less by a Greek philosophical conception (spirit and matter eternally opposed to each other), but by the teaching of the Word of God.

Let no one think we are out of those woods. If you want to measure the strength of the docetic view in the Christian community today, count the homes, Sunday School classrooms, church windows, and illustrated devotional literature in which Hoffman's picture of Jesus praying in Gethsemane appears. He kneels devoutly before a rock in the garden, hands folded serenely, purple robe trailing majestically from his shoulder, a face of utter tranquility uplifted bathed in rays of heavenly light. However horrible the hours that impend, the bitterness of the cup he must drink, the loneliness, the hellish irrationality of it all, he is unperturbed, calm, the self-possessed master of the situation. Only the thorn branch extending artistically into the picture suggests that somehow something might be wrong. That is a sample of Christian docetism in the twentieth century which is more taken with a romanticizing perversion of Gethsemane than with the plain teaching of the gospels.

The question must be asked: Does the Word of God written sustain the same relationship to other literature as the personal Word made flesh sustains to our humanity? Has the Word of God entrusted to prophets and apostles become human literature in the same sense in which the eternal Logos became a human being? The answer to these questions, at least from the Reformed segment of the church, has been a definite Yes. Its practice of these answers has not always been as positive as its theological affirmations have been, but it is with these affirmations that we are concerned.

It is the teaching of Reformed theology that in the manner in which the eternal Son of God became fully man, even to the point of emptying himself of his divine glory without surrendering his deity—in that same way and to the same extent God's self-revelation to man in its inscripturated form is fully human writing while at the same time being and remaining without diminution the full and unqualified Word of God. That is the far-reaching meaning of the Reformed doctrine of organic inspiration.

The classic Reformed formulation of the humanity of the Bible must be credited to the distinguished Dutch theologian Herman Bavinck. For three quarters of a century his teaching has stood theologically unchallenged in the Reformed community. He wrote:

> The *Logos* has become *sarx* [flesh] and the word has become Scripture. They are two facts which not only are parallel, but also most intimately related. Christ has become flesh.... In the same way has the word-revelation of God entered the sphere of the creaturely, the life and history of peoples and nations, in all manner of dreams and visions, research and reflection, even to the point of the humanly weak and despised and ignoble; the word became inscripturate and has as a piece of writing subjected itself to the vicissitudes of all human writing... the scriptures are the product wholly and entirely of the Spirit of God who spoke to the prophets and apostles, and at the same time are wholly the product of the activity of the writers (*Gereformeerde Dogmatiek*, 2nd ed., 1906, Vol. I, pp. 459, 460).

The Bible therefore is as fully and truly a human book as Christ was fully and truly a human being. As the Son of God became human and lived his humanity from crib to cross to the point of limited knowledge, temptation, and death, so the Word of God written is a human book, the product of thought, investigation, planning, and composition like any other piece of literature. We don't have a docetic Christ and we don't have a docetic Scripture.

The Bible, consequently, is not only the Book that stands as a judge and illuminator of all other books. It is also, and as really, a book among books. As such it may be analyzed and studied like all other literature in order to establish for men today the meaning that it had for its writers and their readers in their time. True, only the eye of faith can discern this meaning, but this meaning can never be ascertained apart from its human expression and form. It is in this respect also a true counterpart of the Word become flesh:

> He came to his own home, and his own people received him not. But to all who received him, who believed in his name, he gave power to become children of God; who were born, not of blood nor of the will of the flesh nor of the will of man, but of God (John 1:12, 13).

The humanity of Christ and the humanity of Scripture both hide and reveal the divine reality that found embodiment in the creaturely form. This has deep implications for the practice of biblical criticism.

There is a hiatus to be bridged between the original manuscripts of the Bible and the copied manuscripts which we at present have. The bridging of that gap is the task of lower or textual criticism. But there is an equally significant gap between the way the writers' contemporaries were expected to read these writings and the manner in which we, after more than nineteen centuries, can understand them. The bridging of this cultural, literary, historical, social, religious, and other kind of gap is the task of higher criticism.

Speaking about the higher criticism of the Old Testament, James Orr wrote in his central article "Criticism of the Bible" in the *International Standard Bible Encyclopaedia*:

The gains that have accrued from it on the literary side in a more exact and scholarly knowledge of the phenomena to be explained (e.g. distinction in the divine names; distinction of the P element in the Pentateuch from that known as JE) are not to be questioned; on the historical and religious sides also, much has been done to quicken interest, enlarge knowledge and correct older ideas which have proven untenable—in general, to place the whole facts of the Old Testament in a clearer and more assured light.

An example of such helpful use of higher critical methods in the study of the Old Testament is found in the dating of Ecclesiastes by the late Professor E. J. Young in his *Introduction to the Old Testament.* Young's concern for the integrity of the Bible as the Word of God needs no mention in evangelical circles. Even among conservative theologians he stood if anything to the right of center in his evaluation of liberal higher critical study of the Bible. Nevertheless, he judged that the writer of Ecclesiastes lived at the time of Malachi (about 450 B.C.) and " placed his words in the mouth of Solomon, thus employing a literary device for conveying his message." The ground for this judgment is that "the language and diction of the book apparently point to a time later than that of Solomon" (p. 340). In view of the claim of the writer that he is "the son of David, king in Jerusalem," who surpassed "all who were over Jerusalem before me,"* which for centuries led the church to consider Solomon to have been the author, we have in Professor Young's analysis a case of pure higher critical interpretation.

*In the 1949 edition. The revised edition, 1960, pp. 368, 369, omits the first quotation, "who placed his words . . .," but the time of writing remains unchanged.

It constitutes a higher critical application of the dictum of Professor Louis Berkhof quoted near the end of Chapter 3 above, "It is hardly necessary to add that the textual critic may not allow himself to be influenced by traditional views or by any dogmatic presuppositions."

A contemporary apologete of note for the integrity of the Bible as revealed Word of God is the British theologian J. I. Packer. In his book *God Has Spoken* he writes that the "critical" movement

> squares more easily with a naturalistic, evolutionary, anti-miraculous, uniformitarian outlook than it does with any form of the belief that biblical and church history has actually been *caused* by repeated intrusions (revelatory, miraculous, regenerative) of the power of God in new creation. . . .

This might seem ground enough to shun higher criticism as a method of studying the Bible. But that is far from being the case. Packer goes on:

> The use of an historical method of studying Scripture is a theological necessity nonetheless. For God's revelation really did take the form of an historical process. . . . The reality of biblical inspiration does imply that we learn God's message through finding out what the writer meant . . . and unless we understand their statements historically . . . we are bound to misunderstand them more or less. . . . Historical criticism, then, though in the past abused, is really essential; there can be no good commentaries or accurate exposition or sound theology without it. We do well to remember at this point that the proper meaning of criticism is not *censure*, as such, but *appreciation* (pp. 61–63).

In short, higher criticism is a necessary tool in the study of the Bible and is demonstrably fruitful. There is no difference *of any kind* between higher criticism, systematic theology, or exegesis as legitimate theological activities. All three can be and have been used with great blessing for the church; all three can be and have been used destructively. The discipline as a technical academic activity is neutral. You do not have to read far into John Macquarrie's *Principles of Christian Theology* to discern that it is cast in the form of Heideggerian existentialism. But we do not therefore surrender systematic theology to the philosophers. All things are ours, whether Paul or Apollos or Cephas or the world or life or death or the present or the future, or lower or higher criticism, all are ours; and we are Christ's, and Christ is God's.

We must in conclusion note more specifically than we have the very important *functional* difference that exists between lower and higher criticism. From a *formal* point of view both disciplines are at one in making critical judgments about the Bible. Their respective *functions*, on the other hand, are very diverse. The judgments made by lower criticism are far more objectively bound than are those of higher criticism. The area within which the textual critic must make his judgments is limited by the available textual manuscript material. While his task cannot well be performed without resort to higher critical considerations, such use is ancillary to his basic specifically textual interest. He works, as we have seen, with objective and agreed norms which not only contain but are intended to contain his subjective judgments.

The case is quite different in higher criticism. While the higher critic is deeply interested in the accuracy of the text, his overriding concern is to shed light on what the author meant when he wrote the text. The many interconnections which existed between Israel and its environment and between the New Testament church and its environment inevitably lead to studies in the history, literature, religion, art, philosophy, and the social and political relationships of the respective periods. The necessity of such study cannot be denied, but obviously it is not subject to the same kind of objective norms that govern lower criticism. A humanistic critic will inevitably have his studies of Israel's religion profoundly colored by his presupposition that the human spirit cannot be affected by revelation of the divine. He must see everything in terms of intracosmic forces. This is precisely what happened in the heyday of such criticism in the nineteenth and early twentieth centuries. The Christian critic will equally be influenced by his belief that God does reveal himself to man. The presupposition of the humanist and the belief of the Christian are both prescientific dispositions of their heart and mind. They are not determined by their scholarship but by forces working in them that establish their basic attitudes to ultimate reality. Working with the same data they come to disparate conclusions as to their meaning. Nevertheless, as Packer correctly points out, the abuse of higher criticism, however great it has been, does not undo the fundamental principle that the Bible as literature, as history, as a record of religious teaching, ritual, and practice, may and should be studied comparatively.

The humanistic higher critic is by no means dead. But there now stands over against him a phalanx of expertly qualified Christian higher critics who are able to meet him fully and fearlessly on his own ground. Humanistic higher criticism, while not acceptable in its religious conclusions, has produced masses of valid data which it would be quite wrong for the Christian critic to ignore or to refuse to incorporate into his own research and analysis. Here, too, the word of the Preacher remains true: "For to the man who pleases him God gives wisdom and knowledge and joy; but to the sinner he gives the work of gathering and heaping, only to give to one who pleases God" (Eccl. 2:26).

With these basic considerations before us we are in position to examine specific scriptural data which invite higher critical evaluation.

CHAPTER FIVE

Infallibility and the Gospel Record

If you ask the average Bible reader what the differences are between Matthew, Mark, Luke, and John, he would be hard put to tell you. He might remember a few things of note: that Matthew and Luke have birth accounts of Jesus and that Mark and John do not; that the Sermon on the Mount is found in Matthew; that Mark is the shortest of the four. After some further thinking he might recall that our Lord's high-priestly prayer is found in John and, of course, John 3:16 is found in John.

For the rest the four gospels appear as a sort of blur to our average reader. Every book says pretty much the same things found in the other books but in a different kind of way. What the average Bible reader seems to be saying in this is that none of the four gospels seems to have, so far as he can see, a distinctive personality of its own. He is always meeting an account called "the gospel." He is always hearing some sort of composite melody called "the gospel." He has never really met Matthew as *Matthew*, Mark as *Mark*, Luke as *Luke*, or John as *John*. All he knows is "the gospels."

This is not wholly the fault of the reader. Approximately ninety percent of Mark is substantially found in Matthew; and about fifty percent of Mark is found in Luke. In both cases this is often word-for-word or nearly so. A similar relationship exists between Matthew and Luke, in which Mark is not involved at all. As a result the first three gospels are called the Synoptics, that is, they see things as one or they see things together. Even John may leave at least the superficial impression that he is looking together with them. This would, however, be a very inadequate way of describing John.

These similarities have been a problem in the church almost from the beginning. About A.D. 170 a certain Tatian, probably a Syrian Christian, tried to blend all the gospels together in a harmony called the *Diatessaron* (meaning "the Fourfold"). This he did with considerable skill. He wove passages ranging from parts of a verse to whole paragraphs into one continuous account divided into fifty-five sections. Below follows a sample passage, with references, about the death of John the Baptist:

And his disciples came and took his body, and buried it. And they	Mark 6:29
came and told Jesus what had	Matt. 14:12
happened. And for this cause Herod said, I beheaded John;	Luke 9:9
who is this of whom I hear these things? And he desired to see him. And Jesus, when he had	Matt. 14:13a
heard, removed thence in a boat to a waste place alone, to the other side of the Sea of Galilee,	John 6:1
which is the Sea of Tiberius.	

Natural though such a blending of the four gospels may seem to be, it is neither good nor excusable that this be done. God has given us four gospels, not one. We should not magnify existing similarities between them into an elimination of distinctive differences.

Although the *Diatessaron* went into eclipse, Tatian's idea of one conflated gospel has never wholly left the church. In the sixteenth century so great a theologian and commentator on the Bible as John Calvin wrote a commentary on Matthew, Mark, and Luke, in which all similar passages were printed and explained together. Where there were differences, it was or was not noted but, in any case, differences in such an undertaking are inevitably minimized.

It should give pause for thought that the books God has given us about the words and deeds of Jesus do not come through with more distinctiveness than they do. But really, in terms of the traditional "evangelical" attitude to the Bible, why should the four gospels come through individually? Are they not all "God's Word"? What difference does it make whether Mark or Matthew speaks that word? The lip service given to the "individuality" of the writers is inherently incapable of combating this leveling tendency. So the blur remains.

The reason is not far to seek. For the average devout Bible reader the humanity of the sacred writings is *docetic.* They present themselves as human, but in fact this is not thought to be very relevant. What really counts is that they are "God's Word." It is seldom *Matthew's* word. So why bother about Matthew? Or Mark or Luke or John? The humanity of the Bible is not denied, but neither is it taken with radical seriousness. That God very clearly chose to have the ministry of our Lord presented from four distinct points of view is not regarded as of fundamental importance. We continue to labor under the *Diatessaron* type of mind.

It does not lie within the scope of our discussion to pursue this concern further. We must surrender it for a more fundamental aim, namely that of fostering an attitude to the reading of the Bible that will bring into larger focus than is now the case the humanity of the canonical writings. Unless this is done, God's Word will never speak its full message to us. We must try to see the Bible not as we want to see it or as we have been trained to see it, but as God has very clearly and very plainly been pleased to give it form and character. If this is to be done fruitfully we must come to terms with higher criticism. We must come to terms with it technically and interpretatively at the academic level, and, in due course, popularly for the devout but theologically unschooled body of Bible readers.

We shall take the subject up not by writing abstract essays about "higher criticism" but by taking common-sense note of a number of problem passages in the Synoptics. But first, a word about the Synoptics as a unit.

We have indicated that there is a substantial literary base which contributes to the blur experience in the average Bible reader's perusal of the gospels. How does this come about?

It has already been noted that almost the whole of Mark is substantially found in Matthew and half of it in Luke. As a result there are scores of passages (pericopes) that Matthew, Mark, and Luke have in common. There are a number of others, however, that only Matthew and Mark share, and similarly a number that only Luke and Mark share. Further, there is a large body of material that Matthew and Luke have in common. Finally, all three, but especially Matthew and Luke, report events and sayings that are found in neither of the other two. In short, if we call Matthew, Mark, and Luke A, B, and C respectively, we find this: there are reports shared by A, B, and C; by A and B; by B and C; by A and C; and finally, there are reports by A, B, and C individually.

It is the overwhelming view of New Testament scholars that Mark is the basic source of Matthew and Luke. This source has been supplemented by other sources less identifiable. How to understand in which way the complex skein of cross references came into being is called the synoptic problem in New Testament studies. It tries to account for the interrelationships of the three gospels to each other, the distinctive characteristics of each, and to note the varying contexts in which these relationships and characteristics come to expression.

The synoptic problem cannot be seen in anything like its full dimensions without the use of a harmony of the gospels, in which the parallel passages are printed in columns alongside each other. The similarity, diversity, and unity which such a reading reveals is nothing less than baffling, amazing, and marvelous. The more one concerns himself with it the more he discerns a majestically patterned mosaic in which the divine and the human blend in an organic unity to bring into being the beauty of the Word of God in the literary garment of man.

Our interest at this time is to look at a number of parallel passages and note without further comment their distinguishing characteristics from a literary and content point of view. From the viewpoint of the traditional teachings of verbal inspiration and infallibility these are problem passages, and their movement is in an ascending order from the very elementary to the more complex.

The Marcan column should be read first and then the variations should be noted from this pericope in those of Matthew and Luke. It will often be hardly less revealing to compare Matthew and Luke in their variations from each other. All quotations are taken from the British Revised Version (1885), of which the Standard Version is the American counterpart, as they are reproduced in H. F. D. Sparks' *A Synopsis of the Gospels*. In the introduction to this book Sparks points out that the Revised Version is a very literal translation and is therefore lacking in the literary quality of some other versions, but that in a synopsis this is a virtue, because such a translation more faithfully reflects the order and choice of words in the original Greek.

What we intend in all this is to look at the similarities and differences in the gospels as we would in noncanonical writings that are literarily closely related to each other. In this chapter we shall cite examples in which we simply make the differences explicit. In a later chapter we shall look at the reasons for these differences.

Matthew 3:11	Mark 1:7, 8	Luke 3:16
	And he preached, saying,	John answered, saying unto them all,
I indeed baptize you with water unto repentance:		I indeed baptize you with water;
but he that cometh after	There cometh after me	but there cometh he

Matthew (cont.)	Mark (cont.)	Luke (cont.)
me is mightier than I, whose shoes I am not worthy to bear:	*he that is mightier than I, the latchet of whose shoes I am not worthy to stoop down and unloose. I baptized you*	*that is mightier than I, the latchet of whose shoes I am not worthy to unloose:*
he shall baptize you with the Holy Ghost and with fire.	*with water; but he will baptize you with the Holy Ghost.*	*he shall baptize you with the Holy Ghost and with fire.*

These passages are representative of the remarkable way in which substantial sameness finds diverse expression. Mark unites the baptizing with water and the baptism with the Holy Spirit. Matthew and Luke separate them with the shoes reference. Matthew's reference to the shoes, however, is markedly different from the one shared by Mark and Luke. Notably, Mark does not have the reference to the baptism with fire.

Matthew 20:29, 30	Mark 10:46, 47	Luke 18:35–38
And as they went out from Jericho, a great multitude followed him. *And behold, two blind men sitting by the wayside. . . .*	*And they come to Jericho: and as he went out from Jericho, with his disciples and a great multitude, the son of Timaeus, Bartimaeus, a blind beggar, was sitting by the wayside. . . .*	*And it came to pass, as he drew nigh unto Jericho,* *a certain blind man sat by the wayside begging. . . .*

This incident is remarkable for two rather striking differences in the accounts. Matthew and Mark agree that it occurred when Jesus *departed* from Jericho. Luke reports it as happening when he *approached* the city. Matthew reports *two* blind beggars to be involved, Mark and Luke *one*. The first disparity can be explained by the first two lines in Mark. Luke could easily have mistaken Mark's "they come to'' for his more relevant ''as he went out.'' Both Matthew and Luke omit the name of the blind man.

Matthew 20:20–28	Mark 10:35–45
Then came to him the mother of the sons of Zebedee with her sons, worshipping him, and asking a certain thing of him. *And he said unto her, What wouldest thou? She saith unto him, Command that these my two sons may sit, one on thy right hand, and one on thy left hand, in thy kingdom. . . .*	*And there come near unto him James and John, the sons of Zebedee, saying unto him, Master, we would that thou shouldest do for us whatsoever we shall ask of thee. And he said unto them, What would ye that I should do for you? And they said unto him, Grant unto us that we may sit, one on thy right hand, and one on thy left hand, in thy glory. . . .*

Matthew (cont.)	Mark (cont.)	Luke 22:24–27
And when the ten heard it, they were moved with indignation concerning the two brethren. *But Jesus called them unto him, and said, You know that the rulers of the Gentiles lord it over them, and their great ones exercise authority over them. Not so shall it be among you: but whoever would become great among you shall be your minister; and whoever would be first among you shall be your servant.*	*And when the ten heard it, they began to be moved with indignation concerning James and John. And Jesus called them to him, and saith unto them, Ye know that they which are accounted to rule over the Gentiles lord it over them. . . . But it is not so among you: but whosoever would be great among you, shall be your minister;* *and whosoever would be first among you, shall be servant of all.*	*And there arose also a contention among them, which of them was accounted to be the greatest.* *And he said unto them, The kings of the Gentiles have lordship over them; and they that have authority over them are called Benefactors. But ye shall not be so: but he that is the greater among you, let him become as the younger;* *and he that is chief, as he that doth serve.*

These pericopes constitute a more complex form of similarity-divergence. In Mark the request for a position of honor is made directly by the two brothers. In Matthew it is made through the mediation of their mother. Luke does not report the request at all. Since Mark may be assumed to have made the original report, one wonders why Matthew introduced the mother. Luke joins Matthew and Mark in reporting Jesus' rebuke. There is, however, a marked peculiarity about Luke's record of Jesus' rebuke. While Matthew's report is obviously of one piece with that of Mark, the occasion in Luke is altogether different. There is no request for a place of honor. The unedifying scene which he reports took place at the last supper. The scene in Matthew and Mark is on Jesus' journey from Galilee to Jerusalem. Luke therefore transposed the words of Jesus not only to an entirely different situation, but to a time at least some weeks later.

Matthew 19:9	Mark 10:11, 12	Luke 16:18
Whoever shall put away his wife except for fornication, and shall marry another, committeth adultery.	*Whoever shall put away his wife, and marry another, committeth adultery against her: and if she herself shall put away her husband, and marry another, she committeth adultery.*	*Everyone that putteth away his wife, and marrieth another, committeth adultery: and he that marrieth one that is put away from a husband committeth adultery.*

The exceptive clause in Matthew makes his position on divorce an essentially different one from that of Mark and Luke. According to them the marriage bond is not dissoluble. Divorce is forbidden without qualification. Matthew, on the other hand, twice states (cf. 5:32) that the marriage bond is lawfully dissoluble if fornication has taken place.

Matthew 28:6, 7, 8	Mark 16:6b, 7, 8	Luke 24:6–9
He is not here; for he is risen, even as he said. Come, see the place where the Lord lay . . .	*He is risen; he is not here: behold, the place where they laid him! . . .*	*He is not here, but is risen:*

Matthew (cont.)	Mark (cont.)	Luke (cont.)
and lo, he goeth before you into Galilee; there shall ye see him. . . .	*He goeth before you into Galilee: there shall ye see him, as he said unto you.*	*remember how he spake unto you when he was yet in Galilee, saying that the Son of man must be delivered up into the hands of sinful men, and be crucified, and the third day rise again.*
And they departed quickly from the tomb with fear and great joy. . . .	*And they went out and fled from the tomb; for trembling and astonishment had come upon them. . . .*	*And they remembered his words, and returned from the tomb. . . .*

When one reads these three passages uncritically he is almost bound to overlook a far-reaching difference between them. Matthew and Mark have virtually identical accounts. Luke, however, skillfully puts the word "Galilee" into a context which has a wholly different reference. In Matthew and Mark "Galilee" has a future reference, and it has to do with a meeting with Jesus. In Luke "Galilee" has a past reference to a prophecy which Jesus had made about his suffering. By his reference to Galilee he keeps a verbal resemblance to Matthew and Mark at the precise point at which they use the words in their accounts. Yet he makes it the occasion for a completely different reference. And with good reason. Matthew, and Mark by clear inference, ascribe post-resurrection appearances in Galilee to Jesus. In Luke the disciples not only do not leave Jerusalem but are commanded by the risen Lord not to leave the city until the coming of the Holy Spirit (24:49b).

Finally, we wish to note a remarkable difference between the Synoptics collectively and the gospel of John. In the synoptic version virtually the entire ministry of Jesus, so far as its temporal extent is concerned, takes place in Galilee. Mark is perfectly representative: Jesus goes to Galilee in 1:14 and returns to Judea and Jerusalem in 10:1. Luke has a long account of the return journey extending from 9:51 to 19:27, but it does not change the basic synoptic pattern. Shortly after Jesus' return to Jerusalem his conflicts with the Jewish leaders precipitate his arrest, trial, and crucifixion. In John the account of Jesus' ministry bears no resemblance to this. His preaching base appears to be Jerusalem from which he occasionally goes north to Galilee. Going to and returning from Galilee are found in 1:43 and 3:22, and in 4:2 and 5:1. In 6:1 Jesus is found in Galilee with no reference to his departure from Jerusalem. In 7:10 Jesus returns to Jerusalem, but privately, not openly as in the Synoptics. After this John does not report Jesus as being in Galilee until after his resurrection (ch. 21). Notable in this disparity is the cleansing of the temple which in the Synoptics takes place at the end of Jesus' ministry but in John at the beginning.

It should be noted, however, that certain synoptic passages seem to require Jesus' presence in Judea for which the synoptic travel account does not appear to have room. (Notable are Mark 14:49, Matthew 23:37, and Luke 4:44.) Luke's reference is very enigmatic. His words, "And he was preaching in the synagogues of Judea," stand in the midst of a detailed report of Jesus' preaching ministry in Galilee. The lament over Jerusalem in Matthew with its "How often would I have gathered your children together" and Mark's "Day after day I was with you in the temple teaching" have no framework within which such action can be placed in the uninterrupted ministry in Galilee as they report it.

It may well be that we should consider John's chronology of Jesus' ministry as in some sense complementing that of the Synoptics. It is, however, quite another question how verbal inspiration and the generally held conception of scriptural infallibility can be made to square with the existing rather massive differences.

In the next chapter we shall analyze in some detail a notable example of such differences as we have here briefly reported. Later we shall discuss the relationship of these differences to our common confession of the infallibility of Scripture.

CHAPTER SIX

The Rich Young Ruler

When we read the synoptic gospels through the glasses of comparative study few parallel passages reward study more than do the three that record Jesus' conversation with the "rich young ruler." The reports of this incident are remarkably similar. They illustrate, however, the extensive differences that seemingly uniform reports can contain. For convenient reference we have printed the three accounts in parallel columns, with problem areas printed in italics.

Our analysis may well begin with the title history has given this well-known incident. It relates the story of the "rich young ruler" who came to Jesus to ask him an altogether crucial question. One would have to look far to find a better illustration of the uniform "blur" with which the synoptic gospels strike most readers. Mark, who must be regarded as the major source of Matthew and Luke, does not call the person concerned young, nor does he designate him as a ruler. He refers to him simply as "one" in the Greek, which the Revised Standard Version quite properly translates as "a man." Matthew modifies this to a "young man." Luke calls him "a certain ruler." All three evangelists agree that he was wealthy. So in the best *Diatessaron* conflating style (cf. the preceding chapter) Mark's "one" has become the much more concrete and attractive "rich young ruler." It is possible of course that the "one" could be a young man, but we have no reason to believe that Mark had this in mind. It is also possible that the "one" could be a ruler, but we have no reason to believe that either Matthew or Mark had that in mind. Nor do we have reason to believe that Luke considered his ruler to be a young man.

We must pass on to more difficult matters. There are two to which I wish to call attention. One is the significant change in the manner in which Jesus answered the young man in Matthew as compared to the report of Mark and Luke. The other is both Matthew's and Luke's omission of Mark's report that Jesus, looking upon the man, loved him. The reports are as follows:

Matthew 19:16–22	Mark 10:17–22	Luke 18:18–23
	And as he was setting out on his journey, a man ran up and knelt before him, and asked him,	
And behold, one came up to him, saying,		And a ruler asked him,
"Teacher, what good deed must I do, to have eternal life?"	*"Good Teacher, what must I do to inherit eternal life?"*	*"Good Teacher, what shall I do to inherit eternal life?"*
And he said to him, "Why do you ask me about what is good? One there is who is good. If you would enter life, keep the commandments. . . ."	*And Jesus said to him, "Why do you call me good? No one is good but God alone.* You know the commandments. . . ."	*And Jesus said to him, "Why do you call me good? No one is good but God alone.* You know the commandments. . . ."
The young man said to him,	And he said to him,	And he said,
"All these have I ob-	"Teacher, all these	"All these have I ob-

Matthew (cont.)	Mark (cont.)	Luke (cont.)
served; what do I still lack?"	have I observed from my youth."	served from my youth."
	And Jesus looking upon him loved him,	And when Jesus heard it,
Jesus said to him, "If you would be perfect, go, sell what you possess. . . and come, follow me."	and said to him, "You lack one thing; go, sell what you have . . . and come, follow me."	he said to him, "One thing you still lack. Sell all that you have. . . and come, follow me."
When the young man heard this he went away sorrowrowful, for he had great possessions.	At that saying his countenance fell, and he went away sorrowful; for he had great possessions.	But when he heard this he became sad, for he was very rich.

As Mark and Luke relate the story, a man (a ruler) comes running to Jesus, kneels before him and asks, "Good Teacher, what must I do to inherit eternal life?" Jesus says to him, "Why do you call me good? No one is good but God alone. You know the commandments. . . ." Matthew reports it qu e differently. A young man comes to Jesus and asks him, "Teacher, what good deed must I do, to have eternal life?" To which Jesus replies, "Why do you ask me about what is good? One there is who is good. If you would enter into life. . . ."

What is striking here is Matthew's rewording of Jesus' answer to the man as reported by Mark. Luke, on the other hand, takes Mark over almost verbatim. "Rewording" is not too strong a description for what Matthew does at this point. And, more particularly, his rewording is not innocent. He does not report the same thought in different words. Jesus' answer to the young man's question as reported by Matthew is *substantively* different from Jesus' answer in Mark and Luke.

In Mark and Luke, Jesus simply answered the man's question in terms of the common view concerning Jesus that existed in the Jewish community, namely that he was a rabbi, a teacher of religion. What Jesus said to the man was: Don't rate your teachers too highly. Only God is really good. No reflection was intended here, as some have held, on Jesus' consciousness of his sinlessness. The man addressed him as a teacher in Israel and Jesus answered him in terms of that assumption. The still less defensible view that Jesus was here denying his deity arises from an unnatural, uncontextual reading of the situation in which Jesus spoke. But how some interpreters understand Mark is not our concern at this point. Our interest is in why Matthew substantively reworded Jesus' answer as first given in Mark. It is the more in order to ask this question because Luke, as we have seen, took Mark's report over almost word for word.

To see the extent of the change Matthew effected, we must consider the wholly different use to which he put the word "good." In Mark it is twice applied to Jesus and once simultaneously to "no one" and to "God." This is done in the words "*good* teacher," "Why do you call me *good?*" and "No one is *good* but God alone." In Matthew it is applied to God as it is in Mark, "One there is who is *good.*" But it is not applied to Jesus at all: "What *good deed* must I do?" and "Why do you ask me about *what is good?*" Matthew retains the adjective in the man's words but transfers it from modifying Jesus to modifying a work worthy of meriting eternal life. In response to the question Jesus becomes rather philosophical and asks why the young man is concerned "about what is good." The shift in the reference of "good" from Jesus to a more or less abstract quality of goodness is too noticeable to be ignored. Further, Matthew softens Mark's "No one is good but God alone" to "One there is who is good." Why did Matthew effect this change in wording and in meaning?

There is a school of thought which reasons that Mark, writing in the late sixties of the first century, could speak much more freely about Jesus' humanity than could Matthew, whose writing is placed in the eighties or even later. Mark's writing stood closer to Jesus' earthly ministry in time, and he had known Peter well and doubtless many other eyewitnesses of Jesus. While his book clearly affirms Jesus' divine sonship and assumes it throughout, he also wrote about him as Jesus' own generation viewed him. The theologizing process of relating Jesus' two natures to each other had not yet begun. He therefore saw no incongruity in Jesus' perfectly natural remark as a rabbi in Israel: "Why do you call me good? No one is good but God alone."

With Matthew, so it is held, the situation was quite different. It was written some twenty or thirty years after Mark, and there is no hard and fast assurance that the book as we now have it came from the hand of Matthew the apostle. The Christian community was at that time more aware of the divine-human relationship in Jesus and tended to protect the former at the expense of the latter. This would then be reflected in Matthew's editing of the Marcan account of the conversation between Jesus and the man who sought his counsel. At the same time, the gospel of Mark was then so well established that more extensive alteration than Matthew undertook would have been objected to. Hence the rather forced use of the word "good" in Matthew's account.

Whether this is a valid explanation of the changes effected by Matthew is another matter. The late Professor Ned Stonehouse correctly points out in his *Origins of the Synoptic Gospels* (1963) that if the above explanation is to be accepted it becomes necessary to account for the fact that Luke, who also wrote substantially after Mark, apparently felt no need for revision. Stonehouse observed:

> Luke's modifications do not touch Mark 10:18, and it would therefore appear that the question of Jesus, "Why callest thou me good?" was unobjectionable doctrinally so far as he was concerned. To recognize this with regard to Luke is, to be sure, not tantamount to saying that it could not have been a stumblingblock to Matthew, but it does point up the urgent necessity of exercising utmost restraint in drawing conclusions as to what later evangelists supposedly found objectionable in Mark (p. 96).

Before continuing with the first of our two problems, it will be well, having brought Luke more fully into the picture, to introduce the second problem. This is the omission in both Matthew and Luke of Mark's report concerning the attitude of Jesus to the man who sought his counsel. When in response to Jesus' answer the man said, "Teacher, all these have I observed from my youth," Jesus "looking upon him loved him." The Greek word that Mark uses here (*agapao*) represents the highest designation of love in New Testament writing. If Matthew had difficulty with Mark's "No one is good but God alone," then we can understand his difficulty here for the same reason. Jesus should not show *agape*-love to a man who rejected him. One wonders, however, why Luke omitted Mark's report of Jesus' love response. His acceptance of Mark's "Good Teacher," "Why do you call me good?" and "No one is good but God alone" would presumably dispose him to adopt Jesus' love response also. But this is not the case.

Two possibilities stand open here. Conceivably Luke may have felt that this reference could be eliminated without loss of meaning. The other and more subtle possibility is that Luke was little or not at all disturbed by Jesus' "Why do you call me good?" etc. in Mark's account, but that he drew the line at Mark's report that Jesus loved the man who put his wealth above the love of God. If this is so, then Matthew and Luke would appear to show a common attitude to Mark's frank display of Jesus' down-to-earth humanity. Matthew then took exception to Mark's wording twice, Luke once. There is more to say for this than the three parallel sections alone would suggest.

The alteration in Matthew 19:17 has every appearance of being deliberate. Matthew gives reason to believe that he wanted to change the meaning of Mark's reported answer of Jesus to the man's question as much as possible while changing Mark's words as little as possible. Hence his three uses of "good," as in Mark, only one of which has the same reference as in Mark. The change in the subjects modified by "good" cannot possibly be accidental. Clearly, Matthew wanted to change *something* in Mark's report. Once more we ask, What did Matthew have in mind?

I have already expressed the judgment that two

proposed explanations are not to be entertained. One is that Matthew considered Mark's report to question the sinlessness of Jesus. The other is that Matthew considered Mark's report to question the deity of Jesus. There is nothing in Mark's account to warrant such considerations. If Jesus answered the man in terms of the man's (and the community's) view of him, then there is nothing strange in his reply. We must therefore look for other reasons for Matthew's alteration in Jesus' response, as also for Matthew's and Luke's omission of Jesus' deep affection for the man.

I feel sympathetic, but in a limited way, to the explanation that growing christological awareness in the church led both Matthew and Luke to the changes they effect in Mark's account. What Matthew and, in a lesser degree, Luke called into question, it would appear, was Mark's judgment, his wisdom, the propriety of presenting Jesus so naturally, so frankly, so naively human. Would people in reading such a statement as "Why do you call me good? No one is good but God alone," not be in danger of drawing wrong conclusions from it? Matthew had, we might say, the protective instinct. He probably felt like those who do not know how to handle Hebrews' blunt statements about Jesus' being tempted in the days of his flesh. The omission of Mark's reference to Jesus' love for the man wholly fits into this supposition. In this view, Matthew had two reservations with respect to Mark's report, while Luke had one. Both reservations had the same root: Mark was a bit too blunt about Jesus' humanity.

This view is certainly supported, perhaps altogether justified, by other Matthew-Luke *vis-à-vis* Mark relationships. In 6:1–6 Mark speaks of the offense which Jesus' townfolk took at Jesus' teaching and mighty works, so much so, in fact, that "he could do no mighty work there." This, too, appears to have been a bit too strong language for Matthew. Was Jesus *unable* in any situation to do mighty works? Therefore in the identical parallel context he writes, "And he did not do many mighty works there, because of their unbelief" (13:58). With "did not" in the place of "could not" and "not . . . many mighty works" in the place of "no mighty work" Matthew safeguarded the ability of Jesus to show his power.

In Mark 4:38b, which finds Jesus asleep while a storm on the Sea of Galilee threatens to swamp the boat in which he and the disciples were crossing, the disciples cry out in their fear, "Teacher, do you not care if we perish?" That was not a very complimentary thing to say to the Master, and Matthew and Luke both recognize this. In Matthew (8:25) the anguish of the disciples is no less intense than in Mark, but it is more restrained in its expression: "Save, Lord, we are perishing." In Luke (8:24) the cry is, "Master, Master, we are perishing." In neither of these is there room for any reflection on Jesus' concern for the welfare of his disciples.

Mark apparently regarded the reference to the mother parent alone as adequate to identify Jesus. When Jesus' townfolk took offense at his teaching and mighty works Mark reports them as saying, "Is not this the carpenter, the son of Mary, and brother of James and Joses?" (6:3). Both Matthew and Luke add a reference to Joseph. With characteristic ingenuity Matthew (13:55) changes the reference of carpenter from Jesus to Joseph and thereby alters the report: "Is not this the carpenter's son? Is not his mother called Mary? And are not his brothers James and Joseph. . .?" The "son of Mary" becomes "the carpenter's son." Since the word "son" could not well be used again, its place is taken by "Is not his mother called Mary?" Luke, on the other hand, follows the custom of referring to the father only: "Is not this Joseph's son?" (4:22). In a quite different context, we may add, John takes a mediating position between Matthew and Luke: "Is not this Jesus, the son of Joseph, whose father and mother we know?" (6:42).

Matthew's alteration of Jesus' reply to the young man as reported in the incident of the rich young ruler is textually more far-reaching than the three examples given above, but concern for Mark's freedom in referring to this or that aspect of Jesus' humanity seems to be the feature common to all four sets of changes. It is clear that Luke was as capable of and almost as given to making such alterations as Matthew. Both his and Matthew's omission of Jesus' love for the man which Mark reports are also best explained in terms of the entire context here considered.

The basic problem with which this discussion confronts us is: May one, should one, in a passage in Scripture in which one writer both depends on and diverges from another, resort to a higher critical method in resolving attendant difficulties? What is meant here by "a higher critical method" may be put this way: if one found similar likenesses and differences in three secular writers, and if one knew considerable details about the life-situation, the *Sitz im Leben,* of all of them, how would one go about seeking an explanation? Would one, in terms of an overarching assumed demand for congruity, strong-arm the differences in the texts by forcing on them a harmonistic exegesis? Or would one start looking for circumstances that would reasonably explain what it was that led to the differences observed in the respective writings?

The latter is certainly the method we would follow with respect to any "ordinary" piece of writing. Now it is the position of Reformed theology that from the viewpoint of the full, unreserved human aspect of Scripture all of its writings are in the most complete sense of the word "ordinary" writings. Luke himself encourages us to approach our reading of the gospels in that way:

> Inasmuch as many have undertaken to compile a narrative of the things which have been accomplished among us, just as they were delivered to us by those who from the beginning were eyewitnesses and ministers of the word, it seemed good to me also, having followed all things closely for some time past, to write an orderly account for you, most excellent Theophilus. . . (1:1–3).

The last thing inspiration does or intends is to deprive the canonical writings of their natural, normal, human character, subject in all respects to the laws governing the writers' psychical, moral, spiritual, and rational faculties. What the relationship is between divine inspiration and thoroughly human writing is a matter for careful consideration in the next three chapters. I wish now to emphasize that the books of the Bible as a collection of religious writings are as human as *Pilgrim's Progress, Paradise Lost,* or Spurgeon's *Sermons.* If this is *not* true, how do we explain that the early church or substantial sections of it for a time held books to be canonical which in the end came to be regarded as not canonical; or that other books at first regarded as not canonical came later to be regarded as canonical? Martin Luther's famous reservation with respect to the canonicity of James was only a final, centuries-long-delayed doubt.

The views set forth above would seem to fit well with the principles laid down by the study committee of the Christian Reformed Synod of 1972 in its report on the "Nature and Extent of Biblical Authority." It says, with special reference to the gospels:

> If the gospels are interdependent one attempts to answer questions concerning differences by analyzing the intent of the author and/or the situation of those for whom he is writing (*Acts,* p. 518).

Commenting on the differences in the accounts concerning the rich young ruler, the report states,

> Here again it is possible to give reasons for the changes found in Matthew's account which are related to the type of audience for which he is writing. To prevent the conversation from being misunderstood, Matthew already interprets it in the form of presentation rather than by attaching a commentary to it (p. 519).

The committee might or might not agree with the particular interpretation I give to the phenomena in question. The exegetical principle underlying my interpretation, however, would seem to be wholly consonant with the committee's position. We have to do, therefore, not simply with events *as such*, but with events *as interpreted* by the canonical writers. The written word of the evangelists is itself an interpretation of the event as it originally took place.

> It is our opinion that this approach—so long as it functions within the framework of the gospels—is permissible within our confession concerning the authority and reliability (infallibility) of Scripture. For it seeks to understand the kind of reporting the gospels themselves indicate, and it does this by observing the similarities and differences the gospels themselves contain (p. 520).

The task of biblical criticism is to ascertain not how inspiration annuls this human quality of the writers, but how it uses it. Inspiration is not organic "up to a point." Inspiration is *always* organic, that is, always congenial in its operation to the divine Revealer and to the human receiver of the revelation. It is always effected *by* the divine Logos *in* a human logos existing in the image of its archetype. It always mediates a revelation spoken in heaven and heard on earth, declared above and believed below, and written by men who were controlled by the Spirit sent by the Incarnate One.

CHAPTER SEVEN

The Infallibility of the
Bible and Higher Criticism

It is relevant at this point in our discussion to take up the question of the Bible in its relationship to biblical criticism. Indeed the foregoing chapters have given urgency to this question. This is particularly true for those who would designate their theological outlook as evangelical or conservative or orthodox. Readers who believe that the question of the infallibility of the Bible has been answered in the negative in the preceding chapters are invited to tune in. They may discover that the matter is more problematic than they think.

The church has always confessed the infallibility of the Bible. It is God's very Word. This at once lends an absolute quality to its truth-character. As deity is of the essence of the Word of God incarnate, so infallibility is of the essence of the Word of God inscripturate. The prophetic message of the Old Testament and the apostolic witness of the New have been inspired by the Holy Spirit of truth and are therefore the unbreakable, ever true Word of the living God.

In the Reformed tradition this truth is well articulated in Article 7 of the Belgic Confession:*

> We believe that those Holy Scriptures fully contain the will of God, and that whatsoever man ought to believe unto salvation is sufficiently taught therein. For since the whole manner of worship which God requires of us is written in them at large, it is unlawful for anyone, though an apostle, to teach otherwise than we are taught in the Holy Scriptures....
>
> Neither may we consider any writings of men, however holy those men may have been, of equal value with those divine Scriptures.... Therefore we reject with all our hearts whatsoever does not agree with this infallible rule.

It should therefore be a matter of some concern that a number of people prefer other words to the adjective "infallible" to set forth this quality of Scripture. I have in mind especially the two words "reliable" and "trustworthy." One meets them again and again in contemporary evangelical discussions about the Bible. An infallible message is, of course, a reliable and trustworthy message. But a

---

*The Belgic Confession was written in 1561 by Guido de Brès, a minister in the Reformed Churches in the Netherlands (who died a martyr six years later), to refute the charge that adherents of the Reformed faith were rebels who rejected the true Christian doctrine according to Scripture. The Synod of Dort (1618–19) made some revisions in the text and adopted it as one of the doctrinal standards of the Reformed Churches. Though it is not widely known outside of the churches in this tradition, I have cited it here as a representative statement from a classical source of the Reformed doctrine of Scripture. Readers may find it enlightening to compare this statement with the formulations in other Reformation confessions; for example, that in Chapter I of the Westminster Confession (1647).

reliable and trustworthy message is not necessarily an infallible one. The difference between infallibility on the one hand and reliability and trustworthiness on the other is the difference between the absolute and the relative. We should therefore be very careful how we use these qualities to define the integrity of the Scriptures.

The ambiguity that has entered the orthodox or evangelical qualification of the Bible is no mere accident. Indeed, there are very deep roots for it. There is a reason for the receding into the background of the word infallible as applied to Scripture and the rising into prominence of trustworthy and reliable. The reason is none other than the legitimate claims of higher criticism. This relationship must be somewhat explored.

In the course of this century, evangelical scholarship has increasingly acknowledged the legitimate place of higher criticism in the study of the Bible. In my own denomination the 1971 and 1972 reports on "The Nature and Extent of Biblical Authority," prepared for the Synod of the Christian Reformed Church, provide a striking illustration. The impact of higher criticism on the thinking of the authors is clearly evident. Scholarly integrity has therefore made it necessary to face rather frontally the fact that many data in Scripture are not in harmony with each other. We cited a number of rather notable examples of this in Chapter 5 and presented a more extended description of one such datum in the preceding chapter.

As a result evangelical scholarship finds itself in a dilemma. The churches it serves have traditionally adhered to the view that the Bible as God's Word cannot contain inconsistencies or disparities of any kind. When disparities appear they must in some way be harmonized out of existence. It is in this sense that the words infallibility and inerrancy are usually applied to Scripture, not only popularly but also theologically. To suggest that there are discrepancies or inconsistencies in the Bible would offend the religious mind of many theologically unschooled believers and some (a dwindling number) of those who have been theologically trained.

The evangelical scholar cannot ignore this. But he also has his academic conscience and the general academic theological community to live with. He resolves the conflict by bowing verbally in both directions. This he does by using the words infallibility, reliability, and trustworthiness interchangeably. The lay mind in the denomination to which the evangelical scholar belongs will probably assume that reliability and trustworthiness mean the same thing as infallibility, and the scholarly sector within and outside his church are silently invited to suppose that infallibility really means reliability and trustworthiness.

Such ambiguity in the use of words has two very serious disadvantages. In the first place, in so high a matter as the proper understanding of the nature of Scripture, usage like this is conducive neither to theological clarity nor to theological integrity. We should therefore seek to avoid it. The second disadvantage is the considerable danger that using "infallibility" in the sense of reliability or trustworthiness will result in losing the quality of absoluteness that attaches to the concept of infallibility. Since absoluteness is obviously not an aspect of reliability and trustworthiness as such, the relative concept will tend in course of time to absorb, neutralize, and eventually eliminate altogether the absoluteness that is implicit in infallibility. The democratizing of royalty will not make kings of commoners but it will very likely pull down royalty to the level of the commoners.

The word "inerrant" is also a misleading adjective. It connotes the unqualified absence of inconsistency or disparity of any kind whatever with respect to any data found in the Bible. Unlike reliability or trustworthiness it is an absolute word. But its absoluteness is applied to an aspect of Scripture that is not in fact inerrant. The Bible is infallible; it is not inerrant in the accepted sense of the word.

With these distinctions before us, what must we understand by the infallibility of the Bible? Here it is important to note that the traditional understanding of infallibility is by no means confined to the harmony or harmonizability of data in the several books of Scripture. It far transcends this popular understanding. Deeply imbedded in the historic view of the infallibility of the Bible is the idea, the massive idea, of the unbreakable, ever valid revelation of the creation, redemption, and consummation of all things in Christ who is himself the Creator, the Redeemer, the Consummator. We must distinguish between these two kinds of infallibility. The untenability of the popular concept threatens the integrity of the scriptural conception. We wish therefore once more to call attention to this in terms of data adduced in earlier chapters.

1. That Jesus *left* Jericho and was appealed to by *two* blind men (Matt. 20:29, 30) is not the same as his leaving Jericho and being appealed to by *one* blind man (Mark 10:46–49) or as his *entering* Jericho and being appealed to by *one* blind man (Luke 18:35–39). That Jesus is the compassionate Savior who responds to all who call on him is the common and abiding teaching.

2. That the mother of James and John asked for a place of privilege for her sons (Matt. 20:20–28) is not the same as the direct appeal for privilege by James and John themselves (Mark 10:35–45). And the way in which Luke used Jesus' answer to them (22:24–27) relates to a context quite different from that in which Matthew and Mark place it. That Jesus calls for a greatness whereby the kingdom of God inverts the values of the kingdom of man is the common and abiding teaching.

3. That there should be no divorce at all (Mark 10:10–12; Luke 16:18) is not the same as the teaching that there is the one ground of adultery for divorce (Matt. 5:32; 19:9). That marriage is of God's own making and that he enjoins its sanctity on all is the common and abiding teaching.

4. The words spoken by the angel to the women at the tomb of the risen Christ (Matt. 28:6–8; Mark 16:6b) are in an important respect not reconcilable with the words spoken to the women by two angels in Luke 24:6–9. That Jesus truly rose from the dead is the common and abiding teaching.

5. The place given to Judea in the ministry of Jesus according to the gospel of John can hardly be squared with the exclusiveness with which Galilee is made the focal center of Jesus' ministry before the

Passion in the Synoptics. That Jesus taught the Kingdom of God as he walked among men in Galilee and in Judea is the common and abiding teaching.

6. The question of "the rich young ruler" and Jesus' response to it in Matthew 19:16, 17 is substantively different from the question and answer reported by Mark (10:17, 18) and Luke (18:18, 19). That Jesus taught people to love God above all and their neighbors as themselves is the common and abiding teaching.

The question arises: Are we going to make the effectiveness of our witness to the truly scriptural infallibility of the Bible depend on our ability to harmonize such data? When the data cannot reasonably be brought together, must we then appeal to the no longer existing original documents with their assumed correspondence in all respects? Or must we, as in the case of Jesus' cleansing of the temple, which John places at the beginning of Jesus' ministry and the Synoptics place at its very end, say that there were *two* temple cleansings? The very most that can be said here is that there *may have been* two temple cleansings. But that helps us not at all. Infallibility has no room for a "may have been." Infallibility declares "thus says the Lord." When we must reconcile disparities by constant and often artificial harmonizations, and by sundry assumptions, our witness to the infallibility of Scripture is bound to create a credibility gap.

Should we not rather understand the infallibility of Scripture in such a way that it does *not* include the assumption that all data in Scripture are necessarily harmonizable? In looking for such a conception of infallibility we are not concerned simply to obviate a difficulty. The problem is considerably larger and deeper than that of contriving an escape from embarrassment. The problem is basically that of relating, as essential qualities of the Word of God inscripturate, the divine—which is always absolute —and the human—which is always relative.

Any attempt to articulate the concept of scriptural infallibility will do well to take full note of the relevance of the incarnation of our Lord. In him, in that human being known to history as Jesus of Nazareth, the Second Person of the eternal Trinity was always present, objectively, really, totally present. More than that, the divine presence was constitutive of his human existence. Without the presence of that divine Person in the human being, Jesus would not be Jesus. Yet this deity of our Lord was not *obviously* present, it was not *demonstrably* there. Had the rulers of this world understood the secret and hidden wisdom of God, they would not have crucified the Lord of glory. It must be revealed through the Spirit (1 Cor. 2:6–10). Jesus came to his own home and his own people received him not. But to all who received him, who believed in his name, he gave power to become children of God, who were born not of blood, nor of the will of the flesh, nor of the will of man, but of God (John 1:11–13). It required and requires faith, the new birth, to discern and adore the deity in the humanity.

It is no different with respect to the objectively existing infallibility of the Word of God. When belief in the gospel opens one's eyes to the eternal

God speaking through the Scriptures, those very words which to the unbelieving are simply religious literature (even sublime religious literature) are seen to be the infallible Word of the ever-living God. Such faith overleaps all inadequacies of human expression, all literary, cultural, numerical, geographical disparities, gaps, inconsistencies. Faith embraces the Word that speaks with the certainty, the assurance, the infallibility of God's covenant address to humankind.

This conception, it must be emphasized again, is not a new understanding of the doctrine of the infallibility of Scripture. For the believing community this view of infallibility has *always* existed. It is not a latter-day definition of the integrity of Scripture. It is simply the application to the Bible of Jesus' age-old saying, "Thy Word is truth."

Even so, there *is* a new element in this view of infallibility and it is of great importance. The new element consists in an absence, an excision. It excludes from the understanding of infallibility the conception that the Bible as a human literary product is a book in which literary, historical, geographical, numerical, or other disparties *do not* and *cannot* exist. In that sense the Bible *cannot* be said to be infallible or inerrant. The true infallibility of Scripture is an article of faith. "He who is of God hears the words of God; the reason why you do not hear them is that you are not of God" (John 8:47). Like the existence of God, the fact of creation, the nature of man as image-bearer of God, the reality of God's covenant, the deity of Christ, the atoning power of his death, the fact of his resurrection, the coming of the Holy Spirit, the nature of the church as the Body of Christ, the present reality and future revelation of the new age, the infallibility of the Bible cannot be demonstrated, cannot be proved. It can only be believed, experienced, known through one's acceptance of the gospel of Christ.

The adoption of such a view of infallibility as its exclusive meaning will put many things into proper focus and perspective. It will relieve the Christian mind of a great deal of tension that is not only painful and unnecessary but also without merit or inherent justification.

1. When discoveries in the area of general revelation as disclosed by science, history, or other disciplines call into question certain data of Scripture or certain views we have held about them, the Christian with a true view of the infallibility of Scripture will not be disturbed. Nor will he be unduly elated when such research vindicates the truth of some disputed statement in the Bible. General revelation and special revelation both have one and the same Author. The Creator God *is* the Redeemer God and the Redeemer God *is* the Creator God. The two are not competitors for our loyalty, love, and devotion. The Christian who understands that will patiently await the results of sifting and verification, and when this process has resolved itself his esteem for the Creator who redeems and for the Redeemer who created and re-creates can only be enhanced.

2. The adoption of the scriptural view of infallibility will from a comparative religion point of view set the Bible free from an unwholesome, fruitless, and hopeless competition with the Qu'ran, the holy

book of Islam. There indeed is a writing which according to the received Muslim teaching is literally infallible, verbally and factually inerrant. From a higher critical point of view nothing is more far-fetched than this claim. Some day Islamic scholarship will have to go through the agony of coming to terms with this incontestable reality. Until that (possibly far-off) day dawns, let us hold our view of Scripture as we hold our view of Christ—truly divine and truly human. In our defense of Christianity to the Muslim community let us make plain our view of infallibility and not fear to speak the offense of the literal fallibility of the Bible to Muslims as the church has not feared to preach the scandal of the cross to the Jews.

3. To hold this view of infallibility does not mean that the Christian now surrenders the Bible to the unbelieving higher critic who may without hindrance play fast and loose with it. He who has found and continues to find the Bible to be the living Word of the living God can only hold the Bible in the highest honor as the Book among the books. He will always see the whole of Scripture in terms of the reverent, praising, and adoring esteem of Psalm 119. Standing on this rock that cannot be moved, he can afford fearless honesty in handling the human literary garment that both hides and reveals the infallibility with which the divine Author has spoken to us. In yielding up datings that cannot be defended, in reclaiming dates that had been wrongly surrendered, in acknowledging disparities where they are evident, in seeing a time-conditioned context as the bearer of a verity that cannot change, in seeing redemptive content poured into

secular frameworks, in recognizing Babylon and Egypt, Greece and Rome, mountains, seas and rivers, art and literature, science, religion and history as earthly instruments of heaven's designs, the believing student of Scripture senses ever more profoundly the mystery and the ecstasy of Paul's "O the depth of the riches and the wisdom and the knowledge of God!" as these find specific expression and embodiment in the salvation disclosed to us by the infallible Word.

The infallibility of Scripture which is here proposed is therefore a conception neither broader nor narrower nor in any way different in character from any other doctrine taught in Scripture. It is of one piece with the truths taught in the Apostles' Creed. As it is not possible logically to demonstrate the existence of the Father or of the Son or of the Holy Spirit, or to demonstrate logically the works peculiar to each, so it is not possible to demonstrate logically by proof, either internal or external to Scripture, the infallibility of the Bible. The word of the cross is folly to those who are perishing, but for believers in that word it is the power of God (1 Cor. 1:18). That Psalm 119 is sublime religious poetry is evident to anyone with literary appreciation; what it is really saying can be understood only by one who prays, "Open my eyes, that I may behold wondrous things out of thy law" (vs. 18). No one knows the Son except the Father, and no one knows the Father except the Son and any one to whom the Son chooses to reveal him (Matt. 11:27). If men do not believe Moses and the prophets, neither will they believe though one rises from the dead (Luke

16:29–31). If we had a demonstrably infallible Bible, would it be more effective in our conflict with the world than the ark was that Israel took from the Holy of Holies to do battle with the Philistines (1 Sam. 4:41)? Not by might nor by power shall God's house be built, but by God's Spirit, says the Lord (Zech. 4:1–10). If the gospel is veiled, it is veiled to those who are perishing, but those for whom God has said, "Let light shine out of darkness," receive in their hearts the light of the knowledge of the glory of God in the face of Jesus Christ (2 Cor. 4:3–6). The Pharisees believed in the literal infallibility of the Old Testament, but they did not see the Fulfilment of its promises when he stood before their eyes.

The infallibility of the Bible must be seen as an integral and characteristic part of the majestic movement of God's redemptive enterprise among men concentrating itself in a baby born in a stable. There he put down the mighty from their thrones and exalted those of low degree; there he filled the hungry with good things, but the rich he sent empty away (Luke 1:52, 53). With his priests and scribes, inerrant book in hand, Herod did not understand this (Matt. 2:1–8). The friendship of the Lord is for those who fear him, and he makes known to them his covenant (Ps. 25:14).

Do those who understand these things have to know whether there were one or two temple cleansings? And as for those who do not comprehend them—would they be brought to believe if they were infallibly shown that there were two?

CHAPTER EIGHT

Jesus and the Scriptures

The reflections presented on infallibility make it desirable briefly to consider the authority which Jesus attached to the books of the Old Testament and to his own words as reported in the four gospels. This is the more appropriate because appeal to the authority of Jesus is sometimes made to deprive higher critical study of the Bible of its legitimate place.

It may be said without qualification that Jesus considered the sacred scriptures of the Jewish community authoritative in the highest degree. Again and again he quoted from them. His "it is written" was the end of all argument. His mission was to fulfil the Scriptures. All its teachings led to and focussed on him. "And beginning with Moses and all the prophets, he interpreted to them in all the scriptures the things concerning himself" (Luke 24:27). His almost casual "and scripture cannot be broken" (John 10:35) summed up not only the Jewish community's but also and not least his own view of the august authority of the sacred writings. For Jesus Scripture and Word of God were convertible terms.

Jesus' statement, "scripture cannot be broken," is no more than another way of saying: Scripture is infallible. Here, however, we have to make a choice about the meaning of the expression "cannot be broken." Does it mean infallibility construed as literal conformity of the words written to fact or event? Or does it mean, as understood in chapters 6 and 7 above, infallibility construed as conformity of the words written to truth that only faith can discern? Did the unbreakability of Scripture consist for Jesus in the quality of inerrant propositional statement such as historical and scientific reporting seeks to approximate? Or did, in Jesus' view, the infallibility of Scripture consist in propositional statement couched in the language of faith wherein truth is something more and larger or perhaps even other than the mere wording of the proposition that formulates it? Is it the kind of infallibility that that man recognizes who has prayed: "Open my eyes, that I may behold wondrous things out of thy law" (Ps. 119:18)?

It is certainly clear from Jesus' teaching that his high regard for the sacred writings did not include the idea of their finality and ultimacy. His citing from the Old Testament and then adding "but I say to you . . ." asserted the superior truth and authority of his own word. This was not, however, a matter of clash or contradiction, but of maturation and fulfilment. But if this be true, the unbreakableness or infallibility of the old covenant will have to be an organic conception conformable to the kind of inspiration that brings such infallibility into being. In this conception, as we shall see in the final chapter, there is a large role given to the operations of the Spirit in nature and in history.

Because of this, we invite difficulties of insurmountable proportions with respect to Jesus' use of the Old Testament scriptures if we insist on the tenability of the traditional view of biblical infallibility. This is illustrated by a particular position held by the late Professor E. J. Young. As reported above, Young did not believe in the Solomonic authorship of Ecclesiastes. So far as express statement is concerned, the book itself leaves little alternative to accepting that King Solomon who lived in the tenth century B.C. wrote the book. Nevertheless, on grounds of "language and diction," "political background," and "linguistic phenomena" Young concluded that Ecclesiastes had been written by an anonymous author about the fifth century B.C. The application of these wholly higher critical criteria for ascertaining date and authorship raises no problems except for the fact that Young would not allow similar grounds of language and history to have a voice in determining the data and authorship of the Pentateuch and Isaiah. What was the reason for this?

The reason, in important part, is the infallible authority of Jesus. Jesus referred to what Moses had said in the Pentateuch and what Isaiah had said in his prophecy. Therefore Moses is the author of the Pentateuch and Isaiah is the author of chapters 40–66 as well as the first part of the book. This authority supersedes and nullifies any considerations of language, history, or literary phenomena which the higher critic may legitimately adduce to determine the fifth-century date and non-Solomonic authorship of Ecclesiastes.

Professor Young was very explicit about this. When he was asked, ". . . if somewhere Jesus had referred to Solomon as having said this or that in Ecclesiastes [would] his norms of 'language and diction,' 'political background,' and 'linguistic phenomena' suddenly fall away?'' he replied with a frankness born of deep conviction, ''This can be answered in one word, and the answer is Yes. . . .'' Further, ''If Jesus Christ speaks on any subject, what he says is true, even though at times certain 'evidence' may seem to counter his holy words. . . . The Christian scholar will accept this fact, knowing that Jesus Christ is omniscient''(*Introduction to the Old Testament,* 1949, pp. 339, 340, and the Revised Edition, 1960, pp. 368, 369. Further, cf. my article ''Reformed Scholarship and Infallibility'' in the *Reformed Journal* [Feb. 1961], and the letter exchange between Professor Young and myself in the April issue of that year which was occasioned by this article).

Such a use of Jesus' authority and the consequent apparently arbitrary limitation placed on the validity of higher critical study of the Bible need to be examined. Several factors call for consideration.

1. The traditional view of inspiration and infallibility out of which Professor Young's views arose certainly allows for great divergence between the weight and significance of Jesus' words on the one hand and the weight and significance of others speaking in the Bible on the other hand. It does not, however, allow for the slightest divergence between the authority of the words of Jesus and the authority of the words of others speaking normatively on the score of *factuality.* The whole of the Bible, according to the received doctrine, is verbally

inspired by the Holy Spirit, the Third Person of the Trinity. For this reason the Bible in all its parts is said to be inerrant. As Young himself wrote in the letter in question: "When the Bible says 'Moses wrote' or 'Isaiah spake' that settles the question. Moses did write and Isaiah did speak. A Christian scholar must be guided by the express statements of the Bible." If the matter is as simple and straight-forward as all that, however, why are the data set forth in Ecclesiastes not finally authoritative? It states and it nowhere qualifies the statement, "The words of the Preacher, the son of David, king in Jerusalem" (1:1), and again, "The Preacher sought to find pleasing words, and uprightly he wrote words of truth" (12:10). If a statement from Jesus ends all argument and nullifies considerations of language, diction, political background, and linguistic phenomena, why do not explicit statements verbally and inerrantly inspired by the Holy Spirit have the same authority and effect? Is the Spirit less authoritative than Jesus?

2. It is hardly correct to say that Jesus in the days of his flesh was "omniscient." As the Son of God he certainly has the power of omniscience. But in the incarnation he emptied himself of his heavenly glory (Phil. 2:7) and became as one of us. In a particular instance he himself disowned omniscience. Speaking of the consummation he said, "But of that day and hour no one knows, not even the angels of heaven, nor the Son, but the Father only" (Matt. 24:36).

3. Closely related to this limitation is the fact that Jesus again and again accommodated himself to existing beliefs which we no longer accept in the

then existing form. Notable here is Jesus' accommodation to the popular belief in sheol or hades as the abode of the dead with its two adjoining divisions of gehenna and paradise (Luke 16:19–31). Until critical scholarship began to analyze the composition of the books of the Bible it was generally believed that Moses had written the Pentateuch, and Isaiah all of Isaiah. No valid reason can be adduced why Jesus should not have expressed himself in terms of the common deposit of belief in such matters.

4. It is further to be noted that Jesus left not a single written word to posterity. All that we know of his teaching and of the words in which he expressed his teaching we know through *reports* of the four evangelists. The words of Jesus come to us therefore through the same kind of human medium through which the rest of the Bible comes to us. Their authority, like that of other teaching in the Bible, arises solely out of their character as divine revelation. This revelation was mediated by the Holy Spirit speaking through the human authors of Scripture, and it was mediated in ways past finding out. That is why the gift of faith and the illumination of the Holy Spirit are needed to discern what is the mind of the Spirit. The Spirit within us listening to the Spirit speaking in the Scriptures discloses to us the meaning of the infallible Word. This is simply the application to the reading and study of the Bible of the traditional and proven categories, hoary with Latin age, known as the *testimonium Spiritus sancti internum* in its relation to the *testimonium Spiritus sancti externum*. The sole question here is whether we take our dogma seriously. I

believe we do take our dogma seriously, but only up to a point. That point is where human prudentiality begins to set up standards for the reading and study of the Word of God that are not given or sanctioned by that Word.

Finally, and somewhat separately from the above, we may not fail to note the manner in which Jesus' words have been reported by the four evangelists. This raises the question of Jesus' relationship to his own words and teaching in distinction from his relationship to the scriptures of the Old Testament. If in Jesus' view "scripture cannot be broken," then his "you have heard that it was said to the men of old. . . . But I say to you. . ." (Matt. 5) is even more unbreakable. If this infallibility is to be understood in the traditional sense, however, the words of Jesus as found in the gospels place us face to face with a very problematic view of infallibility. According to Matthew, Mark, and John, Jesus, as we have seen, met his disciples in Galilee after the resurrection. According to Luke 24:49 Jesus immediately after his resurrection instructed his disciples to remain in Jerusalem until the coming of the Holy Spirit. In Acts 1:4 this instruction is repeated. This contradiction is hardly reconcilable with the traditional doctrine of inspiration and infallibility.

The same problem arises with respect to Jesus' teaching on divorce. In Matthew 5:32 and 19:19 he states that adultery is a ground for divorce. According to the teaching of Mark 10:11, 12 and Luke 16:18 there is no ground for divorce at all.

Was the question of the rich young ruler and Jesus' reply to it as reported in Mark and Luke or as reported in Matthew? That is to say, *which of these two sets of question and reply did the ruler and Jesus actually speak?*

A higher critic who does not believe in either kind of infallibility referred to in this book might seek to embarrass us with: Which Jesus are you talking about? The Matthean, the Markan, the Lukan, or the Johannine? The traditional view of inspiration and infallibility has no way to get this challenge off its back. It can only take flight into the area of pious self-contradiction. Those who subscribe to the organic view of inspiration and infallibility, on the other hand, have no problem here. They will ask the questioner what the relevance of his question is to their understanding of Jesus' relationship to his words as reported in the gospels.

What all this means is that the organic conception of infallibility does not, like Hophni's and Phinehas' view of God's presence in the ark, profess to teach that it obviously carries its own validation and can be produced at will. The Scriptures have inherent, objective authority. Its validity is not derived from human recognition of it. The revelatory character of Scripture stands on a par with the manifestation of the eternal power and deity of God in the natural world (Rom. 1:20). But only the eye of faith can discern either of these. The unbelieving, though seeing, are blind. Neither the erudition of the scholar nor the piety of the faithful can make this power and deity evident. Only the faith that has been given is given to know them; and its testimony to them is always a *witness*, never a proof.

CHAPTER NINE

The Spirit's Inspiration

In Christian circles we do not argue with the proposition that God has spoken to men and through men, and that in various ways he has caused that part of his redemptive revelation known as the Bible to become inscripturate. The authoritative book which records this revelation we call, wholly correctly, the Word of God. The specific divine activity through which its several books came into being is called inspiration, and this inspiration we understand to have been an activity of God the Holy Spirit.

On these broad but basic theses there is general agreement in the Christian community. Consensus ceases when we seek further to qualify the inspiration of the Bible. How is it related to the thought, experience, and writing activity of the human authors? What role was played by the religious, cultural, social, historical milieu in which the writing took place? Was inspiration limited to the basic ideas set forth while structure and phrasing were left to the judgment of the writers? Or did the inspiration extend to the subparts and details of the writing? If so, was the inspiration mechanical, verbal, or otherwise in character? If not, what is the relationship of the subparts and details to the major themes?

The answer of Reformed theology to these questions has been that the Spirit's inspiration was organic in charcter. As such, inspiration is regarded as a divine activity which is on the one hand wholly congenial to the character of the divine author and on the other hand wholly confluent with the mental, emotional, and spiritual processes of the human agents whom the Spirit influenced. As the divine and the human are organically related in the Person of our Lord, so the inspiring Spirit associated himself with the conscious and unconscious processes of the human agents whom he directed in ways we dare not define.

This conception has, however, never taken full and consistent hold in the evangelical or orthodox section of the church. It has not even done so in any massive way in the specifically Reformed sector. The usual evangelical view stands closer to that of verbal inspiration than it does to the organic conception. From inspiration so conceived infallibility in the sense of the literal inerrancy of the Bible is deduced. There can be no inconsistency between the many data found in the Bible. God cannot lie. His Word is truth. Heaven and earth shall pass away but his Word shall not pass away. True, there are "problem passages" in the Bible. These, however, may not militate against or be permitted to qualify the inerrancy of the Bible which is deduced from the doctrine of inspiration.

With this the scene is set for an exegesis that is basically an exercise in the reading of the Bible in terms of the received tradition. The scene is also set for the exclusion of any serious critical study of the Bible, for examination in depth of its history, poetry, prophecy, and of its relationship to the environment in which the writers grew up and received their religious, cultural, historical mind-set. When critical or secular scholarship discovers data that support the biblical record, these are widely and gladly used. When discovered data call the biblical record into question at any point, there is no comparable concern to enter into dialogue or to acknowledge fact as fact wherever it may be found. The historic evangelical view of Scripture therefore takes no serious account of the findings of higher criticism except insofar as these are compatible with its basic presuppositions. Fortunately for the enrichment of the evangelical mind this compatibility is rather sizable.

The fundamental reason for the continued power of this historic view is the reluctance of evangelical theology (and of evangelicals in general) to give full weight to the doctrine of creation and its implications for God's activity in history and in nature. It is not adequately appreciated that the redemptive activity of God does not take place in a vacuum but operates wholly within the context of creation. Its creaturely instruments—whether men or forces of nature or processes of history—flow out of the basic structure of the created world. God's Holy Spirit continues to move on the face of these waters. The end of God's redemptive activity is not a totally new, wholly unexperienced, absolutely other dimension of existence than that to which we are used.

The new heaven and the new earth which God

will one day bring into being are not in that absolute sense new. The new world is not so much new as restored, redeemed, reclaimed, and thereby vastly enriched. The I that makes me me is the I that, reborn and sanctified, will inhabit the new world. There is indeed a profound *discontinuity* between the world that is and the world that is to be. But equally profound is the *continuity* between the old creation and the new. Indeed, the discontinuity rests upon and derives its significance from the primal work of the Creator which he never cast off but rather revived, resurrected, healed, and made serviceable again to his divine purpose. All dissimilarity, however vast, between the now and the then exists within a basic context of sameness and identity. The catastrophe of death does not alter the obvious meaning of Jesus' promise, "Truly, I say to you, today *you* will be with *me* in Paradise" (Luke 23:43).

It is therefore not surprising that there is a powerful linkage between the work of the Creator God in things natural and the work of the Redeemer God in things spiritual. The one identical God both creates and redeems. The one Logos made the world and became incarnate in it for its salvation. The only Holy Spirit who moved on the face of the primal cosmos to give it life works in the hearts of men to give them new birth in Christ.

It is a misreading of the Spirit's inspiration of the Bible to fail to see it as an activity closely related at basic levels to what may be called the general operations of the Spirit. There is but one Holy Spirit and he operates at all times in the integrity and wholeness of his Person. Our analysis of his works may distinguish between natural and spiritual dimensions, between general and special operations, but these may never be so construed that one aspect works in isolation from the other. The Creator God *is* the Redeemer God and the Redeemer God *is* the Creator God. How often does not a prayer that is intensely spiritual in its concern receive an answer involving all manner of purely natural and secular agency.

Nature and history are not only the stage on which the drama of redemption is enacted, they are also the indispensable condition and instrument of redemption. Israel's homeland was the crossroads of ancient civilizations. It was not an accident that took Joseph to Egypt and made that great country and its Pharaoh the occasion for the profoundly important event called the Exodus. Out of Egypt God called his Son. Jesus was not born in a timeless moment of transcendent history but in a definite year in the Roman reckoning of time and when the greatest of Rome's Caesars ruled the empire. And Jesus began his ministry not in another transcendental moment but in the fifteenth year of Tiberius Caesar, Pontius Pilate being governor of Judea and Herod being tetrarch of Galilee. The entire history of the church is a history in which kingdoms, commerce, wars, earthquakes, famines, powers, principalities, and the rise and fall of empires form the context in which the perfecting of Christ's body takes place. For that very reason all power in heaven and on earth has been entrusted to the glorified Incarnate One.

Is it therefore seriously to be entertained that the

sacred writings which constitute God's redemptive revelation in Scripture sustain no very important relationship (or none at all) to the constant intertwining of the spiritual with the natural and the historical? Was the actual writing of the Bible so totally different from all the flow of human history that it relates and portrays? Israel came forth out of the nations and the nations moved constantly at the periphery of her horizons, at times sustained close relationships to her and made not infrequent incursions into her domain. In Pilate's court the Roman power effectuated the central act that makes the gospel the gospel. If the Holy Spirit worked in history and used history so massively in effecting our redemption, may he not reasonably be expected to work in history and to use history in setting forth the record of his work for our salvation?

True, our reasonable expectations do not determine the *modus operandi* of the Holy Spirit. I believe, however, that the previous chapters have shown that the distinctly human element is everywhere in evidence in the composition of the sacred writings. Not only does the historical dimension appear to play a large part in the composition of the Bible, but so do many other dimensions of created reality. Already in 1906 Herman Bavinck wrote, "Our insight into the historical and psychological mediation of the revelation has only in recent time come to full clarity" (*Gereformeerde Dogmatiek*, I, 456). A great deal has been added to these insights during the nearly three-quarters of a century since then.

The attention the preceding chapters have given to biblical criticism has by that fact focused on the specifically human element in the writing of the Bible. This raises all the more acutely the question: How must we conceive of inspiration as a work of the Holy Spirit? It is not the purpose of this concluding chapter to set forth something like a doctrine of inspiration. Its more modest aim is to point to some characteristics of the operations of the Holy Spirit which must be taken into account in any responsible assessment of his work as inspirer of the sacred writings. These, together with reflections offered above, will carry, I believe, the evidence of their congeniality with the discipline of higher criticism as we have set it forth in earlier chapters. Let us therefore, with the specific work of the inspiration of the Bible in mind, consider some distinctive features of the manner in which the Holy Spirit works.

1. In both creation and redemption the basic work out of which all subsequent operations of the Holy Spirit flow is *the giving of life.* In the beginning he moved upon the face of the cosmic waters. Out of that moving came the ordered life of the world. God breathed (inspired!) into man's nostrils the breath of life and he became a living being. How this cosmic and individual life was conferred we have no means of knowing. Life is the supreme mystery of all created reality. For the same reason we do not know by what process or processes the new life in Christ comes into being. As it is the Spirit who mysteriously constitutes the life of the natural creation, so it is the Spirit who constitutes the life of the new creation. To see God a man must be born again. This new birth is mystery itself. ''The wind blows where it wills, and you hear the sound of it, but you do not know whence it comes or whither it

goes; so it is with every one who is born of the Spirit" (John 3:8). There is therefore nothing that is obvious, self-evident, easily definable or analyzable about the primary work of the Holy Spirit. Yet this primary work conditions all his other works. As the Princeton theologian Geerhardus Vos pointed out: "Life is the term whereby especially St. Paul characterizes all those virtues, graces and dispositions, whether ethical or religious, that the Holy Spirit works in the hearts of men" ("The Eschatological Aspect of the Pauline Conception of the Spirit," in *Biblical and Theological Studies,* by members of the Faculty of Princeton Theological Seminary, 1912, p. 239). We know *that* the Spirit works. We can in various degrees perceive *what* he does. We dare not say *how* he does it. The Spirit's mediation of life eludes observation and analysis.

2. Although the Holy Spirit does not undergo incarnation, his work is a direct continuation of the work of the Incarnate One, builds on it, and brings it to completion. He works incognito. Only the spiritually enlightened eye can see his work for what it is. As we can see life in its manifestations, observe its power, sense its warmth and invigorating strength, but never see life itself, so it is with the Spirit. He hides his divinity, deploys his power in the form of weakness, conquers by gentleness, illumines all things himself unseen. Not by power nor by might does God bring the new creation into being, but by his Spirit. Reticence marks his Person.

3. For this reason the work of the Spirit is seldom demonstrably his work. It expresses itself in an incarnate way. It is the human person who repents, believes, loves, forgives, witnesses, resists sin,

seeks God. It is man who works out all that the Spirit within him effects. Even rebirth is somehow linked up with the hearing of the Word. "The fruit of the Spirit is love, joy, peace, patience, kindness, goodness, faithfulness, gentleness, self-control" (Gal. 5:22). Where do we find this fruit but in the lives of sinful men? All the Spirit's work passes through the prism of lives that are in process of becoming holy. Its pure-light form cannot be seen. The Spirit suffers the perfection of his work to be reflected in the brokenness and imperfection of our lives. If there is one word that most characteristically describes the work of the Holy Spirit in the lives of men it is the word that Reformed theology has chosen to designate the nature and quality of the inspiration of the Scriptures. It is the word *organic.*

We may at this point appropriately recall what we have said before, namely that the Bible as a divine-human book parallels the incarnation of the eternal Son. We have said that, in the same way the Son took on himself our humanity, the Word of God to men took the form of a completely human writing. When we consider the several qualities mentioned above that characterize the Holy Spirit in his relationship to men, what more can we say than that the relationship is indefinable? How shall we define that specific relationship of the Holy Spirit to the writers of Scripture whereby and wherein he mediated to them the Word of God written? We are not without answer, but the answer is of a particular cast. We can say that the inspiration in question was not mechanical, that it was not dictational, that it was not verbal, that it was not merely ideational. But these negatives make no positive contribution to our understanding other than that of protecting the organic integrity of both the communicating Spirit and the recipients of his revelation.

Is it necessary to do more? Again and again we are brought face to face with the fact that the power of the gospel and the efficacy of the Word that declares it to us lie in their incontrovertible reality, not in our ability to conceptualize the reality. Let us turn once more to the incarnation of the Son of God.

There was a long moment in the history of the church when it was tempted to define the relationship between the divine and the human in Christ. The scene was the Council held at Chalcedon in Asia Minor in 451. The *dramatis personae* were the powerful patriarchates of Alexandria, Constantinople, and Rome. Alexandria sought an understanding in terms of subordinating the humanity by fusing it with and merging it into the divine. Constantinople sought to resolve the problem by distinguishing the two natures in a manner that came perilously close to separating them. The Pope of Rome provided the "answer." Against Alexandria he said that the two natures are related to each other "inconfusedly, unchangeably." Against Constantinople he said that the two natures are related to each other "indivisibly, inseparably." The area of positive definition the Council did not enter. In her historic and continuing concern with christological understanding the church has yet to improve on the Chalcedonian discretion.

Wherever the divine and the human meet, there is mystery. And there is also the greatest, the most beautiful, the most satisfying reality: Emmanuel, God with us. In this union of the Son of God with the flesh of our humanity we see at once the deepest divine self-disclosure and the highest human self-realization. In this Holy of Holies of divine-human intertwining we leave our analytic function at the door of the sanctuary and enter only to worship.

It would not seem that the Holy Spirit's inspiration of Scripture is any more definable than is the relationship of the divine and the human in Christ. The written Word that finally resulted from this divine-human interaction is a phenomenon that bears all the marks of humanity. When this wholly human phenomenon is viewed by the mind of faith it is seen to bear even more the overwhelming marks of divine provenance. Because of these two dimensions of its being the Bible may be studied, examined, analyzed, tested, compared internally and externally with all the careful boldness and restrained thoroughness that are fitting in pondering the deep things of God. The divine is truth and the divine is holy. The first leaves us no alternative but to press on to fuller understanding. The second lays on us a burden of reverence as we seek to approach closer and closer to the heart of God and to the final meaning of his mighty works.